GETTING ORDINATION RIGHT

*Essential Elements of Ordination
in the Bible and History*

P. STEVEN PAULUS

WESTBOW
P R E S S®
A DIVISION OF THOMAS NELSON
& ZONDERVAN

WestBow Press books may be ordered through booksellers or by contacting:

WestBow Press
A Division of Thomas Nelson & Zondervan
1663 Liberty Drive
Bloomington, IN 47403
www.westbowpress.com
1 (866) 928-1240

ISBN: 978-1-9736-6316-4 (sc)
ISBN: 978-1-9736-6317-1 (hc)
ISBN: 978-1-9736-6315-7 (e)

Library of Congress Control Number: 2019907152

Print information available on the last page.

WestBow Press rev. date: 07/10/2019

Dedication

To Jane, a lovely and faithful companion

In Memory of Ken Swetland, a good friend and gracious mentor

Contents

Acknowledgements

This book is based on my thesis project in the Doctor of Ministry program at Gordon-Conwell Theological Seminary in South Hamilton, MA. The project was completed in 2005. Most of the material is taken from that thesis with some additions and deletions. My original research has been sharpened by experience and discussion in the subsequent years.

My thanks go out to my advisor on the original project, Dr. Ken Swetland of the faculty at Gordon-Conwell Theological Seminary, who encouraged the project from its inception. He graciously consented to write the foreword to this book. His recent passing makes this publication a bittersweet tribute to his encouraging guidance. I also want to thank my students at the Evangelical Theological Seminary in Osijek, whose questions and interaction with the concepts in this book have honed my thinking on the meaning of ministry and ordination over the past twenty-five years.

I also am thankful to the many pastors from Bosnia, Croatia, and Macedonia who have interacted with this material in the Institute for Pastoral Studies seminars which I have been conducting since 2011.

My involvement with the leaders and pastors of Grace Network (Grace Presbytery and Ministries International) since before its inception in 1987 has led me to ask, and helped me to answer, many of the questions addressed in this project. My thanks to these colleagues, who have consistently sought to serve the Lord faithfully, with accountability, and in good conscience for many years.

Thanks also to Jeff Ell and Justin and Nicole Cober-Lake of One Focus Press, who have shown genuine faith and enthusiasm for this project and have assisted greatly in the early stages of editing *Getting Ordination Right*.

Members of the ordained ministry and several denominational judicatories in the Shenandoah Valley of Virginia where I currently pastor have contributed their time and interest by participating in personal interviews that formed the preliminary phase of the thesis project. They include Todd Brown, Owen Burkholder, Ed Fisher, Chip Gunston, Bob Holley, John Lane, John Petersen, David Reid, Clay Sterrett, Paul Walters, and Larry Thomas. Rabbi Joe Blair of the Temple House of Israel, Staunton, Virginia, contributed very helpfully on the perspective of Judaism concerning ordination. I extend thanks for their sincere interest and encouragement. I also recognize that any deficiencies or errors in the text are mine alone.

Chapters Two, Three, and Four of this book, which cover the patterns of ordination in Scripture, were published as an entry in First the Kingdom of God: A Festschrift in Honor of Prof. Dr. Peter Kuzmic, published by the Evandjeoski Teoloski Fakultet, Osijek, Croatia, 2011. I am grateful for permission to republish this material here.

My deepest thanks to my wife, Jane, and my children, Ben, Anne, and Thomas, who have always willingly served the Lord with their husband and father, even when it meant living in difficult circumstances and conditions and leaving familiar places. God has also blessed Jane and me through our sons' wives, Anna and Rachel, and our (so far) seven grandchildren.

Author's Preface

The practice of ordination is a commonplace in the life of every church, regardless of tradition or doctrinal persuasion. Yet it is a practice, or better, a process, which few can describe with much precision. In many cases much guesswork is involved in recognizing and installing church leadership. Remarkably few books have been written exploring the practice, especially when we consider how ordination affects the life of any church or ministry.

Getting Ordination Right: Essential Elements of Ordination in the Bible and History examines the doctrine and practice of ordination from a biblical and historical perspective. In this book, biblical examples of ordination are not limited to ministry within the New Testament Church, but include Old Testament examples of the anointing and establishment of kings and other leaders of Israel. The historical research includes references to canon law; ancient, Reformation, and modern treatises on the subject; and a comparison of Catholic, Orthodox, and Protestant understandings of the doctrine. Through comparison of biblical and historical sources, I've identified six elements essential to the practice of ordination.

My conclusion affirms that ordination is not required for validation of ministry, but is an affirmation of gifts and responsibilities bestowed by the Holy Spirit upon members of the priesthood of believers. Valid ministry is a gift of God; ordination is a means by which the church, through its leaders, blesses and endorses its ministers. The present work focuses on the entire process of ordination, including the identification, development, and establishment of the church's ministers. It is my hope that this book will serve as a guide for free church and non-denominational movements whose ordination practices are less defined than those of other traditions. It includes a chapter of recommendations for an effective process of development and ordination of new ministers.

One major change from the original thesis format is the placement of the literature review as an appendix to this book. The review should prove quite useful for those interested in digging deeper into the theological roots of the ordination process. However, the book can be read and utilized by ordination councils and others without the literature review.

I am indebted and thankful to Scott Gibson who served as my second reader and examiner of the original thesis, for his recommendation of the title I've adopted for the book in its current form (though he's probably forgotten all about that). *Getting Ordination Right* succinctly describes the thrust of the book.

The original title of the thesis was *By What Authority? Essential Elements of Ordination in the Bible and History with Application for the Contemporary Church.* The question of authority to act in God's name as His servant and a servant of the church is a central theme of the book. Thus Ken Swetland's foreword focuses on the issue of authority, a matter foundational to the question of the presence or absence of ordination.

Foreword

When we hear the word *authority*, do we have a common understanding of what the word means? Dictionaries define the word with a range of meanings, but the first definition usually refers to the right of a person to command obedience from others and to make final decisions. But then one wonders: Is this authority delegated by others – e.g., by electing or appointing someone to a position – or is it something inherent in the person, some kind of competence combined with humility (the two traits are not mutually exclusive) that contributes to people seeing this person as a leader?

If authority is positional, does competence in exercising good and proper judgment automatically come with the position? This is especially an important question if a person is anything but competent to meet a need for which the position exists. I think we would doubt the authority of decisions or actions of an incompetent person even if the position itself usually denotes authority. The political world – and the church world as well – is littered with the bones of incompetent people once in positions of authority.

If, however, authority resides inherently in a person who is not in a position that implies authority, does the person really have authority? You may remember the old advertisement for an investing firm that no longer exists: "When E. F. Hutton speaks, everybody listens." This brings to mind a man I know who was a well-respected layman in a church but who held no elected office or position of power, yet when he spoke, everyone listened seriously to what he said. Authority (competence with humility) was simply inherent in who he was. Because people respected his wisdom and integrity, he could say almost anything and people would take it seriously.

In Matt. 21:23, the chief priests and the elders challenged Jesus by asking, "By what authority are you doing these things? And, who gave you this authority?" Clearly Jesus was *acting* with authority – exhibiting authority over disease, nature, and demons and teaching with authority – but he was not recognized as having *positional* authority. Those who had positions of authority lacked the discernment and humility necessary to see the new thing God was doing. Nor did they accept that Jesus *was* God in human flesh.

In today's world, authority is up for grabs. Particularly in the West, authority is often seen only in the eye of the beholder. For example, one evening the news showed an exchange between a reporter and a man as they were leaving the courtroom; a jury had just indicted the man for a crime. The reporter asked why the man did what he did. The man turned and railed at the reporter, "Who gave you the right to question my motives or actions! I am my own authority and only I decide what is right or wrong for me!" And there we have it.

Add to this context the whole idea of *ordination* and the waters can become even murkier. The word *ordain* comes from the Latin word *ordinare* and means "to put in order." The word *ordination* was first used in the 14th century to indicate a certain authority given to clergy who were commissioned to "put in order" the affairs of the church.

But is this "setting apart" something others do to someone, or can it be something one confers upon oneself? I know a pastor who is well-known for his excellent preaching – in fact, I would say he is one of the best teaching preachers I know – but he has not been ordained in the usual sense by any examination or ecclesiastical authority. He simply says that he has been ordained of God to do what he does and the fact that churches have called him to be their pastor confirms this call. In this case, it is not arrogance on his part but a humble conviction of the call of God on his life.

In the film *The Apostle*, Robert Duvall portrays an evangelist who flees from his church ministry after killing the man with whom his wife was having an affair, but who still feels the call of God on his life to evangelize. In his wanderings, in one scene he is seen alone in a fishing pond baptizing himself and then conferring authority on himself to be an "apostle." Is he really?

Even the whole process of ordination – setting apart someone for leadership in the church – is not practiced the same by local churches, denominations, or judicatories. So-called "low liturgical" churches sometimes have only a minimal process for ordination. I almost experienced this myself. When I was a high school senior, my family moved from a Methodist church to a Baptist one. Very early in my time at the new church I "went forward" at a service one evening in response to what I now refer to as the "generic call" to come forward for just about anything; in this case it was "to accept Christ as Savior, or to renew your commitment to the Lord, or to be baptized [and the water was already there and heated in the baptismal], or to declare a call to ministry." I had felt for some time – since junior high school really – that I was indeed called to ministry, but I had never declared it publicly. Since the invitation included my sense of God's calling, I went forward. When I told the minister why I had come forward, he rejoiced with me and stated that he would convene a council within the church later in the week and by next Sunday I would be ordained. He hardly knew me. Was this proper ordination? Even as a teenager, I sensed this was not the way to do it, so I begged deference until after seminary.

While in seminary fulfilling the required field education (the practicum in a local church, as it was called in those days), I served as Youth Director in a Baptist church (not the one mentioned above). It was a wonderful church with loving believers and a dear pastor. The leaders of the church suggested I be ordained there while still in seminary. I agreed, and a regional council of the denomination convened for the examination. During the examination I revealed that although I was a Baptist and held to baptism of believers, I did not think that total immersion was the only way to do baptisms, just the preferred way best to illustrate the death and resurrection of Christ to new and eternal life in him.

The council debated long and hard about whether to recommend me for ordination while I waited outside the room becoming more and more anxious after minutes ticked on, but in the end they did commend me to the church for this, but only after the pastor "instructed" me in a "proper" view of baptism! Weeks went by without the pastor asking to meet. I rather timidly asked him eventually about when we might meet, and he replied, "Oh, don't bother about that; I actually agree with you, but don't tell anyone," and the ordination took place. Was this the way to do it?

Churches who practice a "higher liturgy" and denominational connectedness have a much more rigorous practice of ordination, including written exams about theology, biblical understanding, and church polity. These papers are examined by a mix of people charged with discerning whether the candidate is indeed worthy of ordination. The service of ordination itself is rather elaborate. I was privileged to partake in the ordination of a colleague in such a setting that involved the candidates for ordination lying prostrate on the floor in front of the church chancel while the minister prayed for them. It was humbling and meaningful. Is this a better ordination than what I experienced? No, just different – but I must admit to being a little envious of the dignity and worship portrayed in his ordination compared to mine.

Other issues remain. Is ordination held by a local church or by a judicatory? Is it for life or can it be revoked? If it is revoked, is that done by the church where the person is pastor, or by some higher ecclesiastical authority, or initiated even by the pastor? What happens when the ordained person does not live up to the standards outlined in the Pastoral Epistles for elders and deacons, or commits a sin that dishonors the Lord, or ruins the reputation of the church in the community, or brings dishonor to the gospel of Christ? Is the person still ordained, or does the behavior itself nullify the ordination? If ordination is removed, can it be restored after a due process of repentance and clear evidence of worthiness for restoration? If restoration of credentials is allowed, can the person be restored to ministry in the same church where the offense occurred or must it be somewhere else? Should churches require ordained persons to "renew" their ordained standing as other professions like social workers, nurses, and doctors require their people to keep up to date in renewing their licenses to practice based on new information to help them practice their profession? The list could go on.

Into this context of questions about authority and ordination Steve Paulus comes with his excellent book, *Getting Ordination Right*. It is not intended to answer all the questions I raise, nor is it a manual on how to proceed with ordination by an ecclesial body. It is, rather, a splendid overview of ordination affirming that "ordination to a specific ministry is indeed a legitimate practice of the Christian church rooted in the Bible and history, and that there is a clear pattern of ordination in both the Bible and history. Furthermore, the proper practice of ordination is necessary to the health of the church and its ministries" (p.15).

Thus, the book provides a framework to address the issues I raise above. What Dr. Paulus does is *foundational* to a mature understanding of the historical and biblical importance of ordination and the authority encased in the act of ordination. The book deserves a careful and serious reading. Well-written, scholarly, and pastoral, this work – like no other that I know – serves as a careful and serious exploration of ordination from both a historical and biblical perspective as this one does.

Steve and I have known each other for years. Our relationship began when he was a Doctor of Ministry student at Gordon-Conwell Theological Seminary where I have been a professor for over four decades, and I had the privilege of supervising his thesis. He has been a dean of a seminary in Eastern Europe, where he still travels to conduct seminars for pastors, a ministry he loves and which is effective in helping pastors serve in difficult areas of the world. For over twenty-five years he has pastored churches in the U.S. He knows whereof he speaks, and he does it with care, seriousness, and godly thinking. I hope that you, the reader, will profit from this book as much as I have.

Kenneth L. Swetland
Senior Professor of Ministry
Gordon-Conwell Theological Seminary
March 28, 2017

Chapter One
Questions about Ordination

Is it necessary to be ordained in order to conduct pastoral
ministry in the Christian church? Is ordination practiced in
the Bible, and is there a recognizable pattern of ordination?
What purpose does it serve? Who may receive ordination?
Who may confer it? How is it conferred? What is the role of the
existing ministry or of the congregation in choosing candidates
for ordination? These questions are asked by many church
bodies today, not only in the historic Christian communions,
but especially in the many developing congregations, mini-
denominations, and networks traditionally known as free churches.
For the former, it is a matter of grasping time-honored traditions.
The latter seek clarity, or even legitimacy, especially for pastors or
other ministers serving these churches.

The doctrine of ordination is foundational to questions of
ecclesiology. "In contemporary theology there is no question more
difficult, more controversial or more urgent than the meaning of
the ordained ministry."[1]

Other questions come to mind. Is ordination necessary to
legitimize ministry? Conversely, is ministry legitimate simply
because it is ordained by a church body? As Miroslav Volf states in
After Our Likeness:

---

[1] Herbert J. Ryan, "The Meaning of Ordained Priesthood in Ecumenical
Dialogues," in *To Be a Priest: Perspectives on Vocation and Ordination*, Robert
E. Terwilliger and Urban T. Holmes, eds. (New York: Seabury Press, 1975), 91.

[S]ince the charismata are gifts of the Spirit, the charismata of office can be based neither on delegation on the part of the congregation (as is often asserted in the free church tradition) nor on a sacramental act of bishops (as understood in episcopal churches). If the charismata of office were generated through delegation, they would be reduced to a purely human commission and authorization. If, by contrast, they were to result from a purely sacramental act (either of the universal church or of the local church) the sovereignty of the Spirit would be endangered . . . .[2]

Is Non-Ordination an Option?

Several of the most effective servants of God in Scripture were never ordained through human agency. Moses was not ordained by human authority, but rather responded to the extraordinary call of God at the burning bush. However, he did later appeal to human authority, the elders of Israel, and gained their support in his efforts to win Pharaoh's consent to release Israel from bondage (Ex. 4:29-31). The people of Israel ultimately recognized and followed the greatest of Hebrew prophets.

The prophet Amos declared, "I was neither a prophet nor a prophet's son, but I was a shepherd, and I also took care of sycamore-fig trees. But the Lord took me from tending the flock and said to me, 'Go, prophesy to my people Israel'" (Amos 7:14-15 NIV). He was rejected by the religious establishment of the Northern Kingdom, possibly due to his lack of priestly or prophetic credentials or perhaps because of his origins in the rival Southern Kingdom. The community of the faithful in Israel came to a different conclusion regarding his ministry, placing his pronouncements in the canon of Scripture.

---

[2] Miroslav Volf, *After Our Likeness: The Church as the Image of the Trinity,* Alan G. Padgett, ed. Vol.I in Sacra Doctrina: Christian Thought for a Postmodern Age. (Grand Rapids: Willliam B. Eerdmans *Publishing Company, 1998),* 248-9.

John the Baptist received no formal endorsement from the religious establishment authorizing his ministry. Thus, the religious leaders feared the question from Jesus, "Why then did you not believe him?" (Matt. 21:25 ESV).

The Apostle Paul made it clear that his apostleship was based on a supernatural call and was "not from men nor through man" (Gal. 1:1 ESV). He was later commissioned with the laying on of hands along with Barnabas by the church at Antioch for missionary work among the Gentiles and Jewish diaspora (Acts 13:1-4). He considered the proof of his ministry to be results rather than ceremony. So he wrote to the Corinthians, "You yourselves are our letter of recommendation, written on our hearts to be known and read by all" (II Cor. 3:2 ESV).

"Who ordained you?" is at the heart of the elders' questions to Jesus, "By what authority are you doing these things and who gave you this authority?" (Matt. 21:23 ESV). It can be said that all ministry comes down to this question, which leads directly to the nature and purpose of ordination in the Bible and history.

Though some of God's choice servants never functioned under the sanction of human authority, in many cases ordination is practiced in the scriptures. How was this issue handled in the Bible, and what was its significance? Just as important, how has it been handled in history? The subject produces differences in both opinion and practice.

All kinds of suppositions about ordination abound. It is thought that Jesus ordained his disciples, that the rite has been practiced continuously since apostolic times, that it has scriptural warrant, that it confers on the recipient a special character that remains with him or her for life, that it protects the church from heresy, that only the ordained should administer the ordinances or sacraments, that it transmits grace for office, that it does *not* transmit grace for office, that it conveys authority, that it conveys nothing whatsoever, and so on.[3]

Today's milieu sees many people who serve independently, claiming an extraordinary call of God. Like the prophet Amos or the apostle Paul, their claim of apostleship or ministry is not of man, nor from men. But is this ever legitimate today? If it is sometimes legitimate, is it always legitimate? How do we know? How has this been viewed historically? Are there some circumstances, practical or historical, in which we should expect this kind of immediate calling *without* the confirmation of a community through ordination more than in others? "Even a congregation that has no official officeholders can be a church in the full sense. But no local church can endure over time and remain true to its own calling without at least implicitly recognizing offices."[4] The significant issue of the meaning of ordination in the life of the local church calls for clarification.

The Vocabulary of Ordination

Biblical discussions of the rite of ordination[5] center on several Hebrew and Greek words, especially those that describe the practice of the laying on of hands.[6] But beyond the issue of the rite of ordination, I want to pursue the question of the broader context of ordination – the identification, nurture, and confirmation of

---

[3] Marjorie Warkentin, *Ordination: A Biblical-Historical View*, (Grand Rapids: William B. Eerdmans, 1982), 1.

[4] Volf, 248.

[5] The English term "ordain" comes from Latin "to set in order," "to arrange." "In later Latin they came to mean to appoint to office. Ordain is used to translate up to thirty Greek and Hebrew words." R.P Lightner, "Ordain, Ordination," in *Evangelical Dicitonary of Theology*, ed. Walter A. Elwell (Grand Rapids: Baker Book House, 1984), 801.

[6] For instance, *shith, samakh* (Heb.), and *tithemi, epitithemi tas cheiras, cheirothesia,* and *cheirotoneo (*Gk.). See Warkentin, pp. 9-10, 35-36. Some additional words will be addressed in a later chapter.

spiritual leadership.[7] The concept of ordination is far more than simply the rite.

Ordination is the means by which the Christian community formally recognizes and establishes its leaders, and thus establishes itself. This work will identify the essential elements of ordination. It addresses the issues involved in bringing an individual to a place of recognition within the church community, a process that results in ordination. This study will enable a church to weigh its current practices and compare them to biblical and historic norms. Such practices can be adjusted to strengthen the processes surrounding ordination. Word studies focus on the rite but encompass much more.

The Hebrew word most often associated with laying on of hands in the sense of "ordain" or "appoint" is *samakh*, which signifies "to lean upon, lay, put, uphold, support"[8] or "apply pressure to."[9] This term is used when Moses commissions Joshua as the leader of Israel prior to his death (Num. 27:23). It was later used in rabbinical ordination. "(I)n the Rabbinic literature of NT times the term *samakh* (lit. to "lean upon, apply pressure to"), used to describe the laying on of hands in order to appoint to office, is limited to the sacrificial cult and the ordination of a rabbi. From the rabbinic texts it is clear that the rabbis ordained their disciples to office by the laying on of hands." [10]

Epitithemi tas cheiras (the laying on of hands) is used in the Septuagint (the Greek translation of the Hebrew Bible) to translate

---

[7] The whole area of Christian leadership is a wide-ranging discussion. It's not my intent to address in detail the oft-discussed issues of hierarchy, servant-leadership, anti-leadership and non-leadership approaches to pastoral ministry current today.

[8] R.D. Patterson, entry 1514, *Theological Wordbook of the Old Testament, Vol. II,* R. Laird Harris, Gleason L. Archer, and Bruce K. Waltke, eds. (Chicago: Moody Bibile Institute), 628.

[9] Frank Hawkins, "Orders and Ordination in the New Testament," *The Study of Liturgy,* Cheslyn Jones, Geoffrey Wainwright, and Edward Yarnold, eds. (New York: Oxford University Press, 1978), 296

[10] Ibid., 297.

samakh. Joshua was filled with the spirit of wisdom through this practice when Moses laid his hands on him. "The transferring of this gift took place before the assembled congregation in order to ratify publicly the legitimacy of the succession."[11]

Epitithemi tas cheiras is a primary term used in the New Testament to signify that one has been set apart for a special task (e.g. Acts 6:6; Acts 13:1-3; I Tim. 4:14; II Tim. 1:6). Another term, *kathistemi,* derives its meaning from "to put in place," or "to set in an elevated position, in an office, to install."[12] The future of this term (*katasteso)* is used in Titus, "This is why I left you in Crete, so that you might put what remained into order, and *appoint* (italics added here)elders in every town as I directed you" (Titus 1:5 ESV). In this case the word is normally translated "appoint" (NASB, RSV, NIV). The King James Version uses "ordain," as does the NIV margin.

Cheirotoneo is another word which comes into play in this discussion. Its original meaning, "raising the hand to express agreement in a vote,"[13] indicates a nomination or a selection process. This raises the issue of the role of spiritual authorities as opposed to or in conjunction with the congregation in the selection and confirmation of candidates for church leadership.[14] The word later came to refer to ordination itself.[15]

Early Historical Developments

For the patristic church, ordination was a primary guarantor of legitimacy. Ordination through apostolic succession was considered a necessity for genuine ministry in the post-apostolic

---

[11] Ibid.

[12] Oepke, "Kathistemi," Gerhard Kittel, ed., Geoffrey Bromiley, trans., *Theological Dictionary of the New Testament,* Vol. III (Grand Rapids: Eerdmans Publishing Co., 1965) 444-445. (Hereafter TDNT).

[13] Eduard Lohse, *"Cheirotoneo"* in TDNT, Vol. IX, 437.

[14] Ibid.

[15] Warkentin, 36.

church.[16] Departure from this standard was a mark of illegitimacy.[17] Clement of Rome (*c.* 95 A.D.) was the first to speak of the issue of succession from the apostles when addressing division in the church in late first-century Corinth. After complaining of the sedition against the existing presbyters there, he states in this oft-quoted passage:

> And our Apostles knew through Our Lord Jesus Christ that there would be strife over the name of the bishop's office. For this cause, therefore, having received complete foreknowledge, *they appointed the aforesaid persons, and afterwards they provided a continuance, that if these should fall asleep, other approved men should succeed to their ministration.* Those therefore who were appointed by them, or afterward by other men of repute with the consent of the whole church, and have ministered unblamably to the flock of Christ, in lowliness of mind, peacefully and with all modesty, and for long time have born a good report with all – these men we consider unjustly thrust out from their ministration (emphasis mine).[18]

---

[16] Though, in a counter view, Leon Morris argues that only by the time of Augustine was ordination itself the means of preserving the succession. "Nature and Government of the Church," in *Readings in Christian Theology,* Vol.3. Millard Erickson, ed. (Grand Rapids: Baker Book House, 1979), 314.

[17] Though see Alexander Strauch, *Biblical Eldership*, rev. ed. (Littleton,Co: Lewis and Roth Publishers, 1995), 286, for the belief that appointment rather than a formal ordination was the norm for the church prior to the early second century. The argument seems to turn on semantics. He states elsewhere that "The first Christians were not adverse to simple, public ceremony for appointing or commissioning fellow members to special positions or tasks .... For important events such as the appointment of elders, some kind of public, official recognition of new elders would be necessary" (p.287). A concern about clericalism causes him to use the word appoint and to eschew the word ordain as a corruption (in his view) of several Greek words often translated thus.

[18] "Epistle of S. Clement to the Corinthians" in *The Apostolic Fathers,* J.B. Lightfoot, J.R. Harmer, eds. (London: Macmillan and Co., 1891; reprint, Grand Rapids: Baker Book House, 1956), 32.

Clement does not address the method of appointment in any detail, whether ordination with the laying on of hands or some other means. He nevertheless establishes the concept of succession as one mark of legitimate ministry along with the consent of the church, humility of character, perseverance in the tasks of ministry, and good repute. These additional marks of legitimacy are significant in our search for a pattern of recognition of church leadership throughout the Bible and history, and will be addressed in a later chapter.

Ignatius of Antioch (*c.* 112 A.D.) contributes to the sacralization (or perhaps clericalization) of the church orders with a three-tiered system of ministry. His system requires a single ordained bishop in a given area for the church to function or even exist. This belief became a given of Catholic ecclesiology[19] and, along with succession, served to solidify ordination[20] as an indispensable practice for preserving church order.

Ignatius establishes the single (monarchical) bishop as the means of preserving the spiritual unity of the church. The bishop is joined by presbyters (priests) and deacons, forming the three major orders of ministry in the patristic church. In Ignatius the bishop is seen as the guarantor of the unity of the church. "Be obedient to the bishop and to one another, as Jesus Christ was to the Father [according to the flesh], and as the Apostles were to Christ and to the Father, *that there may be union of both flesh and spirit*" (emphasis mine).[21]

Again, in another letter Ignatius insists on the unifying role of the bishop:

---

[19] Morris, 312.

[20] Thus Irenaeus, "Those that wish to discern the truth may observe the apostolic tradition made manifest in every church throughout the world. We can enumerate those who were appointed bishops in the churches by the Apostles and their successors (or successions), down to our own day.... " *Adv.haereses, III,* in *Documents of the Christian Church,* Second Edition, Henry Bettenson, ed. (London: Oxford University Press, 1963), 68.

[21] "Epistle of S. Ignatius to the Magnesians," *Apostolic Fathers,* 72.

Avoid divisions as the beginning of evils. All of you follow the bishop as Jesus Christ followed the Father, and follow the presbytery as the Apostles; and respect the deacons as the commandment of God. *Let no man perform anything pertaining to the church without the bishop* .... It is not permitted either to baptize or hold a love-feast apart from the bishop. But whatever he may approve, that is well-pleasing to God, that everything which you do may be sound and valid: (emphasis mine).[22]

Here we see the sacralization of the ministry which declares some functions the exclusive province of ordained members of the community.

In succeeding generations the bishop came to be seen as the guarantor of the doctrinal purity of the church. This is seen in Hegesippus (*c.* 175) and Irenaeus, who consider the issue of succession to be a means of preserving right doctrine. In this way, the foundation of apostolic succession was strengthened. The guarantor of proper succession was the bishop through the rite of ordination. This was important because prior to the final establishment of the canon of Scripture, human office was seen as the primary means of preserving truth, at least in the minds of the Fathers.[23] In their view, opposition to Gnostic heretics who claimed "secret" knowledge required duly ordained and established successors of the apostles. These became vessels of both unity and truth.[24] So writes Hegesippus:

The Church of Corinth remained in the right doctrine down to the episcopate of Primus at Corinth. I had converse with them on my voyage to Rome, and we took comfort in the right

---

[22] Ignatius, "*Epistle to the Smyrnaeans,*" c. viii, *Documents,* 63-4.

[23] Irenaeus' Rule of Faith placed traditional interpretation and practice alongside Scripture as the means of establishing the truth of a given doctrine or practice.

[24] Irenaeus in *Documents,* 68.

9

doctrine. After arriving in Rome I made a succession [list] down to Anicetus, whose deacon was Eleutherus. To Anicetus succeeded Soter, who was followed by Eleutherus. In every succession and in every City things are ordered according to the preaching of the Law, the Prophets and the Lord.[25]

Hegesippus links succession with right doctrine.

Later, Cyprian (*c.* 250) insisted on communion with the Catholic bishop of a given city as the only assurance of orthodoxy and thus salvation:

Thence age has followed age and bishop has followed bishop in succession, and the office of the episcopate and the system of the Church has been handed down, so that the Church is founded on the bishops and every act of the Church is directed by these same presiding officers.[26]

He effectively shuts out schismatics who divide from the church and those who violate this episcopal system with his famous dictum, "He cannot have God for his father who has not the Church for his mother."[27] Since membership in the church was based on communion with the bishop, sects and splinter groups were excluded. In this way, Cyprian's ecclesiology gave even stronger weight to apostolic succession and, by implication, proper ordination.

The Donatist controversy (*c.* 305 A.D. and after) addressed the question of fitness to bestow ordination when Caecilian was ordained by *traditores* (those who had apostasized by surrendering copies of Scriptures to authorities during times of persecution).[28] The validity of his ordination was questioned by rivals on the

---

[25] Hegesippus in Eusebius' *Ecclesiastical History,* IV, xxii, 2, in *Documents.* 67-8.

[26] Cyprian, *Epistle* xxxiii.1 in *Documents,* 73.

[27] Cyprian, "The Unity of the Catholic Church, 6" in *Documents,* p. 73.

[28] Jaroslav Pelikan, *The Emergence of the Catholic Tradition (100-600),* Vol. 1, *The Christian Tradition: A History of the Development of Doctrine* (Chicago: University of Chicago Press, 1971), 309.

grounds that the ordaining authorities were unfit to ordain bishops because of their mortal sin.[29] Later, in answer to this, Augustine formulated the doctrine of *ex opere operato:*

> The Augustinian theology of grace . . . (committed) itself to the principle that the efficacy of the sacraments . . . was assured 'ex opere operato,' by the sheer performance of the act, rather than 'ex opere operantis,' by the effect of the performer upon the act. From one perspective, this assured the priority of the divine initiative; for it was God, not the bishop or the priest, who did the baptizing, ordaining, and dispensing of sacramental grace.[30]

This conclusion fortified the sacramental character of the ordination rite. The issue of appropriate, or adequate, ordaining authority is critical to our wider discussion.

Reformation Developments

Today many Protestant and free churches do not acknowledge the classic concept of apostolic succession or the historic episcopate.[31] Ordination took on sacramental character and became a centerpiece of legitimacy in the patristic and medieval church.[32] The Reformation jettisoned the practice of succession for the most part, with the exception of the Anglican Church. In the Reformation, ordination in some aspects lost its sacramental character.[33] The issue of legitimate ordination is at

---

[29] Ibid.

[30] Ibid., 312-13

[31] Morris, 311.

[32] Ibid., 312.

[33] At least some of its sacerdotal character remains in communions where the ministry of word and sacrament is reserved to ordained pastors or ministers of the church.

the root of reconciliation debates between various communions today.[34]

Luther was particularly vehement in his rejection of the sacramental character of ordination.

> Here is the root of the terrible domination of the clergy over the laity.... In sum the sacrament of ordination is the prettiest of devices for giving a firm foundation to all the ominous things hitherto done in the church, or yet to be done. This is the point at which Christian fellowship perishes, where pastors become wolves, servants become tyrants, and men of the church become worse than men of the world.[35]

For Luther the only legitimate use of ordination was for the church to select its preacher.[36] While strongly affirming the priesthood of believers, he does restrict the ministry of the word and sacraments to those duly appointed by the church.

> (W)e all have the same authority in regard to the word and the sacraments, although no one has the right to administer them without the consent of the members of his church, or by the call of the majority (because when something is common to all, no single person is empowered to arrogate it to himself, but should await the call of the church).[37]

Luther maintains a clericalization of the sacraments but softens the power of ordination itself which creates the clerical distinction.

Calvin objected to the doctrine of apostolic succession on

---

[34] See Herbert J. Ryan, "The Meaning of Ordained Priesthood in Ecumenical Dialogues," *To Be a Priest: Perspectives on Vocation and Ordination,* Robert E. Terwilliger and Urban T. Holmes, eds. *op. cit.*

[35] Martin Luther, "Pagan Servitude of the Church," in *Martin Luther, Selections from His Writings,* John Dillenberger, ed. (Garden city, NY: Anchor Books, 1961), 345.

[36] Ibid., 346.

[37] Ibid., 349.

the basis that it no longer preserved apostolic truth. "It follows, therefore, that the pretense of succession is vain, if posterity do not retain the truth of Christ, which was handed down to them by their fathers, safe and uncorrupted, and continue in it."[38] Further, he states "That in the government of the Church especially, nothing is more absurd than to disregard doctrine, and place succession in persons."[39] Calvin possesses a very developed doctrine of calling and recognition of the ministers of the church.

> Therefore, if any would be deemed true ministers of the Church, he must *first* be duly called; and *secondly*, he must answer to his calling; that is, undertake and execute the office assigned to him…. I am speaking of the external and formal call which relates to the public order of the Church, while I say nothing of that secret call of which every minister is conscious before God, but has not the Church as a witness of it; I mean the good testimony of our heart, that we undertake the offered office neither from ambition nor avarice, nor any other selfish feeling, but a sincere fear of God and desire to edify the Church.[40]

The Anglican Church retained adherence to the doctrine of succession (which came to be known as the historic episcopate) but also reflected attitudes about ordination found in the principal reformers. Article XXV of the Thirty Nine Articles of the Anglican Church denies sacramental status to ordination and four other Roman Catholic sacraments. Like Luther, Article XXIII gives authority for ministry in the congregation to those publicly called and sent, denying this right to those who take the prerogative upon themselves.[41]

Contemporary Concerns

---

[38] John Calvin, *Institutes of the Christian Religion,* IV, ii, 2.

[39] *Institutes* IV, ii, 3.

[40] *Institutes,* IV, iii, 10,11

[41] The Thirty-Nine Articles of Religion (According to the American Revision, 1801), John H. Leith, ed. *Creeds of the Churches, A Reader in Christian*

Some feel that the practice of ordination as it emerged in church history was detrimental to the church's actual mission, suppressing community (i.e. "lay") participation in the ongoing life of the church.[42] "The leadership pattern that evolved, and the ordination rites that were formulated to define and protect that leadership, answered the need for stability and permanence, but the church paid highly for its security."[43] It is not my primary purpose to analyze the development of the theology of ordination in church history and the accompanying suppression of "lay" gifts. Rather, I am seeking to discover across biblical, historical, and denominational practice some universal pattern of identifying, nurturing, and confirming gifts for spiritual leadership in the church of Christ.

Today, especially in the developing non-denominational movements, the doctrine and practice of ordination has been lost in the multitude of beliefs, practices, and rites. Does it have any legitimacy in these movements today, or should it be eliminated as one more cumbersome tradition hindering the priesthood of all believers?[44] Or, from a traditionalist perspective, can such an ordination possess any legitimacy since it has been removed from its historical underpinnings? It would be useful to revisit and

---

Doctrine from the Bible to the Present, Third Edition (Atlanta: John Knox Press, 1982), 274.

[42] For instance, "No one needs to be ordained to preach Christ or administer the ordinances. All such concepts are foreign to the New Testament apostolic churches." Strauch, 287; or James Garrett who advocates ordination for the recognition of ministry but sees the rite historically as a means of producing a professional clergy class, *New Testament Church Leadership* (Tulsa, OK: Doulos Publishing, 1996), 171, 199-201.

[43] Warkentin, 48.

[44] On this issue Warkentin lays out a kind of litmus test for the validity of the practice of ordination. "Only if ordination facilitates the legitimate use of authority in the church is it a valid form. If in the laying on of hands there is any attempt (well-meaning though it may be) to manipulate divine authority, whether through succession theory or through delegation of communal authority, the rite of ordination is illegitimate. The practice of ordination with the laying on of hands must be tested by these criteria.," 183

clarify the doctrine of ordination for the church, especially the non-affiliated churches in our day.

It is my conviction that ordination to a specific ministry is indeed a legitimate practice of the Christian church rooted in the Bible and history, and that there is a clear pattern to be found in both sources. Furthermore, the proper practice of ordination is necessary to the health of the church and its ministries. The use of the term *ordination* here includes the communal process of identifying, nurturing, and confirming leadership roles within the church, not simply the rite of ordination.

Many studies or partial studies have been done on the rite of ordination, with emphasis on the laying on of hands by spiritual leaders for the purpose of recognizing or installing ministers. We will not look solely at the rite of ordination, but rather examine the practices which surround the rite. This includes the identification, nurture, and development of spiritual leadership by the community. We will discover and affirm essential principles surrounding the wider practice of ordination. It is hoped that this study can serve as a guide for churches seeking clarity in this matter, and that it will aid all churches in the identification, and empowerment of its ministers.

We begin by taking a representative event in Scripture – the appointment of Joshua by Moses – and compare the procedure used there with other similar ministry confirmation events in scripture. I am referring to this event as Joshua's ordination. All aspects of ordination will not be repeated in each scriptural instance examined, but a general pattern usually practiced will become clear. The instances examined will not be exhaustive, but representative.

After comparing Old and New Testament examples, parallel practices in church history will be analyzed. This analysis will focus on major patristic texts, principal reformers, and confessions. The emergence of clear patterns or essential elements of ordination will serve to guide developing associations of churches and networks.

Chapter Two
Patterns of Ordination in Scripture: The Old Testament

Moses' Appointment of Joshua

The practice of the laying on of hands is found in several places in the Torah.[45] Moses' appointment of Joshua is the clearest example of its use in establishing leadership for the covenant community.[46] In later Rabbinic Judaism this event was seen as a prototype for the practice of ordination within the synagogue community.[47]

> Then Moses spoke to the Lord, saying,
> "May the Lord, the God of the spirits of all flesh, appoint a man over the congregation, who will go out and come in before them, and who will lead them out and bring them in,

---

[45] Everett Ferguson, "Laying on of Hands: Its Significance in Ordination" *The Journal of Theological Studies,* April, 1975, Vol. XXVI, Part 1, 1-12. M.C. Sansom, "Laying on of Hands in the Old Testament," *The Expository Times,* 1983, Vol. 94, No. 11, 323-326.

[46] From here on I will use the term ordination, realizing the problems some will have with the term theologically. Though there are many legitimate objections to the use of the Moses-Joshua relationship as the model for New Testament or Christian ordination I have chosen to use it as a paradigm. Subsequent discussion will bear out its usefulness for such a purpose.

[47] "After the model of the institution of Joshua, and with express appeal to it, the Rabbis developed their own practice of ordination." Eduard Lohse, *"Cheir,"* TDNT, Vol. IX, 429. Also, Arnold Ehrhardt, *The Journal of Ecclesiastical History*, October, 1954, Vol. V, No. 2, 130.

that the congregation of the Lord may not be like sheep which have no shepherd."

So the Lord said to Moses, "Take Joshua the son of Nun, a man in whom is the Spirit, and lay (*samakh*) your hand on him; and have him stand before Eleazar the priest and before all the congregation; and commission him in their sight. And you shall put some of your authority on him, in order that all the congregation of the sons of Israel may obey him . . ."

And Moses did just as the Lord commanded him; and he took Joshua and set him before Eleazar the priest, and before all the congregation. Then he laid his hands on him and commissioned him, just as the Lord had spoken through Moses (Num. 27:15-20, 22-23 NASB).

Now Joshua the son of Nun was filled with the spirit of wisdom, for Moses had laid his hands on him; and the sons of Israel listened to him and did as the Lord had commanded Moses (Deut. 34:9 NASB).

There are six elements of this event, which can serve as a prototype for all ordinations.

1) The first element of ordination as described here is that it is *of the LORD.* That is, the process of confirming leadership is valid insofar as it recognizes God's sovereign role in choosing spiritual leadership. It follows that any process which ignores this element is illegitimate. Moses' actions, including the choice of his successor and the means by which he is set in place and confirmed before the congregation, are at the direction of the Lord himself. "So the Lord said to Moses, 'Take Joshua the son of Nun, a man in whom is the Spirit, and lay your hand on him ....'" (Num. 27:18 NASB). Thus it

was the Lord who directed Moses to take Joshua and lay his hands upon him. [48]

2) The second element of ordination as described here is the *need* for someone to fill a specific leadership role in the covenant community. That is, ordination is not a rite of general purpose, but addresses a specific concern of the community. "Then Moses spoke to the Lord, saying, 'May the Lord, the God of the spirits of all flesh, appoint a man over the congregation, who will go out and come in before them . . . that the congregation of the Lord may not be like sheep which have no shepherd'" (Num. 27:15-17 NASB). Moses' prayer was for a successor who would be seen specifically as a military leader[49] and shepherd.[50]

3) The third element of ordination is the choice of a *suitable candidate*. The issue of character, spiritual qualifications, and experience are of importance here. This aspect of the process addresses the area of recognition, preparation, and experience. Joshua had served closely with Moses over a period of many years in the wilderness journey of the people. He was Moses' aide from his youth (Num. 11:28). He was with Moses on Mount Sinai (Ex. 24:13). He habitually remained near the presence of the Lord at the tent of meeting (Ex. 33:11). He had proven experience as a military leader (Ex. 17:9-14). Joshua was one of the two spies with the good judgment to bring a good report about the land of promise (Num.

---

[48] Both the singular "hand" (v. 18) and the plural "hands"(v.23) are used in this passage. Milgrom argues "Transfer of authority and power can only be performed by the laying on of both hands . . . . In Jewish tradition the laying on of both hands, called *semikhah*, became the rite for rabbinic ordination." Jacob Milgrom, *BmdbrNumbers* in *The JPS Torah Commentary* (Philadelphia: The Jewish Publication Society, 1990), 235.

[49] Ibid., 234-235. "(W)ho shall go out before them and come in before them (is) (a)n idiom that refers to military leadership."

[50] See Baruch A. Levine, *Numbers 21-36* in *The Anchor Bible*, (New York: Doubleday, 2000), 355 for a discussion of the shepherd figure in ancient Israel and the ancient Near East.

13:8, 14:6). Most importantly, in this case, he was "a man in whom is the Spirit." In view of the mentoring process, intentional or not, Joshua has been prepared for this specific, momentous, and overwhelming task.

4) The fourth element of this event is the *role of the existing spiritual leadership*. Moses, the greatest of Hebrew prophets, is the primary human initiator of the process of appointing and recognizing his successor. He recognizes the need for a successor and is inspired of the Lord to pursue the process. Moses' participation is crucial to the legitimacy of the process of establishing Joshua as the new leader of the people. Also present is the other primary office-holder in the congregation, Eleazar, the high priest. The existing spiritual leadership is in agreement and supportive of Joshua in his new role as leader of the covenant people. In a sense they are saying, "It seemed good to the Holy Spirit and to us" (Acts 15:28 NASB).

5) The fifth element of this process is *the rite itself*.[51] There are several elements of the rite which are significant. They are the practice of laying on of hands, the presence of spiritual leaders and congregation, and the effect of the rite on Joshua[52] and his relationship with the congregation.

The practice of laying on of hands has numerous meanings in the Old Testament.[53] In this case, the most significant is the

---

[51] Many works on ordination focus almost exclusively on the rite of laying on of hands, e.g. Warkentin. However, Ehrhardt *op. cit.* considers other elements as well.

[52] Milgrom comments on the transfer of Moses' authority (*hod*), "The exact meaning of *hod* in this context is difficult to determine, since it is Moses who is doing the investing. He is empowered to transfer to Joshua only his authority. But if *hod* refers to Moses' spiritual powers, then only God who has endowed them can transfer them – as He did when He allowed the elders to share Moses' prophetic gifts." Milgrom, 236.

[53] Giles commenting on Daube and *samakh, sim.*, 184-185.

idea of blessing or impartation.[54] As a result of the laying on of hands, Joshua has received not only an emblem of authority (an endorsement) but an actual manifestation of charismatic power. "Now Joshua the son of Nun was filled with the spirit of wisdom, for Moses had laid his hands on him" (Deut. 34:9 NASB).

The presence or endorsement of current spiritual leaders is required for the legitimacy of the whole rite. It provides continuity and stability to the political structure of the community. The presence of recognized spiritual leaders, of itself, lends *gravitas* to the process, and is a required component of ordination.

The congregation as witness and participant is fitting in that the entire process is addressing a need of the community for a shepherd. Their presence is also a confirmation of the legitimacy of the appointment and succession of Moses by Joshua.

6) The sixth element is the *role of the congregation* leading up to the rite and the effect of the ordination itself upon the congregation. The immediate result is the change of Joshua's status in the congregation. The intention of the ordination is "that the congregation of the sons of Israel may obey" him (Num. 27:20 NASB), that is, that they may accept his leadership. The actual result is that "the sons of Israel listened to [Joshua] and did as the LORD had commanded Moses" (Deut. 34:9 NASB). Through the ordination, Joshua's relationship with the congregation has been enhanced and transformed.

Also important is the role of the congregation in Joshua's life and the role of Joshua with the congregation prior to this point. He has already served and exercised a leadership role in the congregation. He is not an unknown to them. His character, service, and development are a matter of record. In some sense,

---

[54] Ferguson, *op. cit.*

the congregation is able to confirm, receive, and recognize Joshua because of their longstanding relationship.[55]

All of these elements serve as a kind of paradigm for ordination and the processes which surround it. It now serves our purpose to examine other Scripture events. Later we will consider the practices and comments of post-Biblical and modern authors as we attempt to build a paradigm or theology for the practice of ordination in the contemporary church. In the following passages we examine the practice of establishing spiritual leadership in light of the Moses-Joshua model. Some of the events will mirror this pattern well. Other passages use only segments of the paradigm, thus showing the fluid nature of ordination. Ordination is not a mechanical process, but a means of recognizing, training, and confirming spiritual leadership.

The Empowering of the Seventy Elders

Throughout the trials of the wilderness journey, Moses' burden was overwhelming to him. During a time of complaining by the Israelites, the Lord initiated a process whereby others might share the responsibility of governing with Moses. Seventy men were taken from among the people. They were empowered by the Spirit, recognized as elders, and helped Moses bear the burden of service. This event, which confirmed new spiritual leadership,[56] possesses some features of the Moses-Joshua paradigm.[57]

---

[55] From a pastoral perspective, the pastor called to a given congregation from without may have to spend years of service before having this kind of reception and trust level with a believing community.

[56] There is some question as to the role of the previous advisors whom Moses had appointed (Ex. 18:25-26). "The rabbis are sensitive to the fact that Moses already had an advisory council of seventy elders at Sinai but claim that they were guilty of unseemly conduct at Taberah (vv. 1-3) and were destroyed by the divine fire." Milgrom, 86-87.

[57] Though this event in Numbers is prior to the appointment of Joshua, it utilizes some aspects of the later Moses-Joshua appointment.

The Lord therefore said to Moses, "Gather me seventy men from the elders of Israel, whom you know to be the elders of the people. And their officers and bring them to the tent of meeting, and let them take their stand there with you. Then I will come down and speak with you there, and I will take of the Spirit who is upon you, and will put Him upon them; and they shall bear the burden of the people with you, so that you shall not bear it all alone."

Also, [Moses] gathered seventy men of the elders of the people, and stationed them around the tent. Then the Lord came down in a cloud and spoke to him; and He took of the Spirit who was upon him and placed Him upon the seventy elders. And it came about that when the Spirit rested upon them, they prophesied . . . Then Moses returned to the camp, both he and the elders of Israel (Num. 11:16-17, 24-25, 30 NASB).

There are some similarities with the case of Joshua's appointment over the congregation. First, the action taken is *of the Lord.* "The *Lord* therefore said to Moses, 'Gather Me seventy men from the elders of Israel'" (v. 16). The empowerment of these individuals is initiated by the command of the Lord.

Then, it meets a *specific need* among the people of God. In this case, the burden is too great for Moses. The purpose of the process with these elders is that "they shall bear the burden of the people with you, so that you shall not bear it alone" (v. 17). These who are already recognized as elders receive an enhancement of their ability to give leadership to the people along with Moses.

The *candidates* are already prepared and have a track record as "those whom you know to be the elders of the people" (v. 16). Their place of leadership among the people is already a given. How they have qualified and the specific activity of an elder of the people at this time are unknown. The descent of the Spirit empowers them for an enhanced ability to function in their leadership role with the same Spirit as Moses.

The *spiritual authority* is Moses, who has heard from the Lord and acts in accordance with His will. Humanly speaking, he initiates the gathering, calls the leaders together, and is the arbiter of the process. It is a sign of solidarity that Moses and the newly empowered leaders return to the camp together (v. 30).

The *rite* is a very simple matter which does not include the laying on of hands.[58] "[H]e gathered seventy men of the elders of the people, and stationed them around the tent" (v. 24). During this simple process there is an impartation of spiritual power similar to that witnessed later in Joshua's appointment. The Spirit that is upon Moses is placed upon these seventy, even two who are not actually present for the ceremony (v. 26). As a result of this gathering at the tent of meeting,[59] they are spiritually gifted[60] for the responsibilities of eldership.

The *relationship with the congregation* changes, or is enhanced, as these men are empowered to assist in bearing Moses' responsibility of governing the people.

The Anointing of David as King

The case of David's anointing by Samuel is not the same as Moses' placing Joshua over the congregation to succeed him after his death. I Samuel is clear that the establishment of a king over Israel is different from any other office held among the people of

---

[58] Contrary to much that is written, the laying of hands alone does not constitute ordination. Other rites are sometimes used, and the laying on of hands can be dispensed with altogether. Ehrhardt *op. cit* addresses this issue.

[59] "It should be noted that the transplanting of Moses' spirit onto the elders must take place at the Tent of Meeting . . . .At any other site but the Tent, observers might attribute the miracle not to the invisible God but to the visible Moses! Only at the Tent upon which the divine cloud descends (v. 25) can God's visible Presence leave no doubt concerning the source of the spirit." Milgrom, 87.

[60] "The elders, gathered around Moses' tent, are possessed by God's spirit, a sign that their selection by Moses is ratified by God." Ibid., 89.

Israel to that time. Nevertheless, there are some parallels to our paradigm for ordination that are worth exploring.

> Now the Lord said to Samuel, "How long will you grieve over Saul, since I have rejected him from being king over Israel? Fill your horn with oil, and go; I will send you to Jesse the Bethlehemite, for I have selected a king for myself from among his sons....
>
> "And you shall invite Jesse to the sacrifice, and I will show you what you shall do; and you shall anoint for Me the one whom I designate to you." So Samuel did what the Lord said, and came to Bethlehem. The elders of the city came trembling to meet him and said, "Do you come in peace?" And he said, "In peace; I have come to sacrifice to the Lord. Consecrate yourselves and come with me to the sacrifice." He also consecrated Jesse and his sons, and invited them to the sacrifice. Then it came about when they entered, that he looked at Eliab and thought, "Surely the Lord's anointed is before Him." But the Lord said to Samuel, "Do not look at his appearance or at the height of his stature, because I have rejected him; for God sees not as man sees, for man looks at the outward appearance, but the Lord looks at the heart." . . . Thus Jesse made seven of his sons pass before Samuel. But Samuel said to Jesse, "The Lord has not chosen these." . . .So he sent and brought [David] in. Now he was ruddy with beautiful eyes and a handsome appearance. And the Lord said, "Arise, anoint him; for this is he." Then Samuel took the horn of oil and anointed him in the midst of his brothers; and the Spirit of the Lord came mightily upon David from that day forward (I Sam. 16:1, 3-7, 10, 12-13 NASB).

In the first place, the rite of establishing the new king is *of the Lord.* "Fill your horn with oil, and go; I will send you to Jesse the Bethlehemite, for I have selected a king for myself among his sons" (I Sam. 16:1). The prophet Samuel is following the explicit instructions of the Lord in initiating the process of anointing a new king. "[A]nd you shall anoint for Me the one whom I designate to you" (v. 3). The divine prerogative is clear throughout the passage, especially as Samuel rejects David's brothers until he is convinced that the Lord's anointed stands before him.

In light of Saul's failure and the Lord's rejection of him, there is a definite *need* to anoint a new king. This is Samuel's specific purpose as he has the sons of Jesse pass before him – that is, to anoint one of them to be the new king of Israel.[61]

There is a *suitable candidate* in the person of David. Not just anyone will do, even from the "right" family. The Lord's chosen candidate alone can be anointed. Samuel is aware of this. Several statements in this passage and after make us aware of David's preparation. Perhaps most important is that somehow his heart is right before the Lord, for "Man looks on outward appearance, but the Lord looks on the heart." Furthermore, he has already provided significant service to the king and kingdom; both his experience as a musician in soothing the demonized Saul and his experience as a shepherd in preparation for attacking Goliath have served as equipping for the tasks of leadership and ministry assigned to him. Of ultimate importance here is that David is "the one whom I shall designate to you" (I Sam. 16:3).

Clearly, there is spiritual authority for the anointing. There was no one of higher stature than Samuel to give credibility and weight to the proceeding. Samuel, as the *existing spiritual leadership*, takes the lead, under God, for initiating the process.

He engages in a *rite* in the presence of the congregation gathered at the sacrifice. "Then Samuel took the horn of oil and anointed him in the midst of his brothers"(v. 12a). In the rite there is also an impartation of spiritual power – charismatic empowerment. "[A]nd the Spirit of the Lord came mightily upon

---

[61] In rejecting Saul, it seems the Lord is not concerned with preserving the *institution* of the hereditary monarchy. Rather, the concern is to have the man of his choice in this position of leadership.

David from that day forward" (v. 12b). This enduement of power becomes evident in David's subsequent life and exploits.

While there is a congregation at this anointing ceremony, their role is somewhat unclear. The brothers are David's competitors for the attention of Samuel. After the event, they don't hide their disdain (I Sam. 17:28-29). Nevertheless, the presence of the Bethlehem congregation is a significant part of the paradigm. But more significant is the role of the absent community of the people of Israel. They will be the recipients of David's kingly ministry. It is they who sing David's praises (I Sam. 18:7), who are pleased with all his actions (18:5,16), and who, after all, publicly accept his royal leadership (II Sam. 5:1ff.). In this way we see the sixth element of ordination, recognition and confirmation of spiritual leadership by the community.

David, Solomon, and Adonijah the Self-Appointed

Another example of royal succession is instructive with regard to our paradigm for confirming spiritual leadership. In I Kings 1, Adonijah has declared himself king. He has mistaken his father David's silence toward his obvious ambition as tacit approval.

> Now Adonijah the son of Haggith exalted[62] himself, saying, "I will be king." So he prepared for himself chariots and horsemen with fifty men to run before him. And his father never crossed him at any time by asking, "Why have you done so?" and he was also a very handsome man (I Kings 1:5-6 NASB).

---

[62] Adonijah's actions amount to self-appointment, (*ani 'emlok*, I will reign). This issue of self-exaltation is at the root of later rejection of the self-ordained for ministry in the church. E.g. The Cambridge Platform, VIII, 1-3. Section 1 reads, "No man may take the honor of a church officer unto himself, but he that was called of God, as was Aaron." Iain Murray, p. 252. Also see Article XXIII of the Thirty-Nine Articles.

In his own twisted way Adonijah followed all the steps of the paradigm, save one. He recognized the *need* for a successor to the aging King David.[63] He saw himself as a *suitable candidate* for the role of king. He was handsome and had a great PR campaign. He interpreted David's unwillingness to cross him as a confirmation of his desires. Perhaps others did also.

He summoned some of the political and *spiritual authorities* to participate in his bid for succession, for "he conferred with Joab the son of Zeruiah and with Abiathar the priest; and following Adonijah they helped him" (v. 7). Note, they are not initiators of the process as true spiritual authorities, but followers of the presumptuous, self-appointed king.

He also was able to form an impressive *congregation* who gladly acknowledged his kingship. "And Adonijah sacrificed sheep and oxen and fatlings by the stone at Zoheleth, which is beside En-Rogel; and he invited all his brothers, the king's sons, and all the men of Judah, the kings servants" (v. 9). While no specific *rite* is mentioned, the sacrifice and feast is a kind of religious acknowledgment of the validity of Adonijah's succession – i.e. a presumption of God's approval.

Of course, what is missing from Adonijah's scheme is the actual approval of God and the participation of the primary political and spiritual authority, his father, King David.

Enter Nathan, Bathsheba, and Solomon. How does Solomon's subsequent enthronement compare with the Moses-Joshua paradigm? After hearing of Adonijah's coup, the aging David takes action. David immediately calls on God as a witness of the rightness of the action he is about to take. "And the king vowed and said, 'As the Lord lives who has redeemed my life from all distress, surely as I vowed to you by the Lord the God of Israel saying, 'Your son Solomon shall be king after me, and he shall sit

---

[63] G.H. Jones, *I and 2 Kings, Vol.* 1 in *The New Century Bible Commentary*, (Grand Rapids: Eerdmans Publishing Co., 1984), 89. According to Jones the king's impotence is grounds for concern about his health and indicates the need for a co-regent.

on my throne in my place;' I will indeed do this day'" (I Kings 1:29-30 NASB).

Shortly thereafter "Benaiah the son of Jehoiada answered the king and said, 'Amen! Thus may the Lord the God of my lord the king say'" (v. 36). At the conclusion of Solomon's coronation, David says, "Blessed be the Lord, the God of Israel, who has granted one to sit on my throne today while my own eyes see it" (I Kings 1:48 NASB). From David's perspective, the *will of God* [64]has been established in the enthronement of Solomon.[65]

As stated above, Israel was *in need* of a successor to David. Solomon was the *appropriate candidate* who would be acceptable to David and his closest advisors, including Nathan the prophet, Zadok the priest, Benaiah, and others (v. 38). They are simply waiting for David's word on the matter. Zadok, representing these *spiritual authorities,* performed the *ritual* of placing Solomon on a donkey,[66] anointing him with oil from the tent of meeting,[67] blowing a trumpet, and shouting, 'Long live King Solomon.' They also seated him on David's throne. They were followed by the *congregation*, "And all the people went up after him, and the people were playing on flutes and rejoicing with great joy, so that the earth shook at their noise" (v. 40). Thus Solomon's coronation follows the essential elements of the pattern found in Numbers.

It seems that the spiritual empowerment often associated with the rite of anointing actually occurs later in Solomon's

---

[64] "The charismatic factor persisted even in an established monarchy; a king was chosen by Yahweh, as is emphasized in I Kg. 2:15." Jones, p. 90.

[65] Contra Jones, op. cit. p. 89 and Walter Brueggemann, *1 Kings* (Atlanta: John Knox Press, 1982) who see a manipulation of the aged and feeble-minded King David. Given the context of the event, this seems unlikely.

[66] "Riding on David's mule was a sign of his royal status. There are frequent references to eminent persons riding on an ass (Jg. 5:10; 10:4) or a mule (2 Sam. 13:29); similarly, the Ugaritic texts describe the king-god Dan'el riding on an ass." Jones, p. 98.

[67] Presumably, oil reserved for the specific purpose of anointing was kept apart in the sanctuary." Ibid., 103.

experience – a kind of delayed effect. In I Kings 3:5 the Lord appears to Solomon to give to him whatever he should ask for. This encounter is the source of Solomon's legendary wisdom, a supernatural enduement of power from God.

Chapter Three
Patterns of Ordination in Scripture:
The New Testament

The Appointment of the Twelve

One of the most significant events in Jesus' ministry for our purposes is the appointment of the twelve apostles. Luke's account is more extensive than those of the other synoptic gospels.

> And it was at this time that He went off to the mountain to pray, and He spent the whole night in prayer to God. And when day came, He called His disciples to Him; and chose twelve of them, whom He also named as apostles ... And He descended with them, and stood on a level place; and there was a great multitude of his disciples, and a great throng of people from all Judea and Jerusalem and the coastal region of Tyre and Sidon (Luke 6:12-13,17 NASB).

> And He called the twelve together, and gave them power and authority over all the demons, and to heal diseases. And He sent them out to proclaim the kingdom of God and to perform healing (Luke 9:1-2 NASB).

The events recounted here are several chapters apart. There is a hiatus between their appointment and empowering. Numerous episodes separate the choosing of the twelve and their preaching and healing mission. Does the appointment of the twelve follow

any of the essential elements we have assigned to ordination –
the process of recognizing, nurturing, and confirming spiritual
leadership?

First there is the question of divine initiative. Is the
appointment *of God?* Of course, in the case of Jesus, recognition of
His divinity requires an affirmative. But in His humanity, does His
night spent in prayer before this significant appointment indicate
a need to discern the Father's will? In this way we can say that
the decision of whom to appoint is ordained of the Father. Though
nothing is mentioned of the purpose of the night of prayer, this is
one possible conclusion. Regardless, since Jesus is the one making
the appointment, these men are made apostles by the will of the
Lord. Mark puts it this way: "And He went up to the mountain
and summoned those whom He Himself wanted, and they came to
Him" (Mark 3:13 NASB).

Is there a *need* for the ministry of the twelve? The multitude
is mentioned in Luke's first passage quoted above. They are in
need of care. Before the preaching mission in Matthew's gospel,
Jesus states the rationale:

> And seeing the multitudes, He felt compassion for them,
> because they were distressed and dispirited like sheep without
> a shepherd. Then He said to His disciples, 'The harvest is
> plentiful, but the workers are few. Therefore beseech the Lord
> of the harvest to send out workers into his harvest' (Matthew
> 9:36-37 NASB).

The extension of Jesus' ministry was a clear need filled by the
appointment and commissioning of the twelve, and later the seventy.

In terms of the question of need, the number of disciples is
significant.

From this larger number of adherents Jesus chose twelve.
This is the number of the tribes of Israel, a number which indicates
that Jesus was establishing the true Israel, the people of God. In
Jesus and his followers "people could see a dramatization of the

Old Testament picture of God bringing the twelve tribes of Israel to the Promised Land" (Tinsley).[68]

Is a *spiritual authority* involved in the appointment? Jesus is *the* spiritual authority, the Messiah of God. To be sure, His authority is not universally recognized (an issue to be examined later), but His blessing is, of course, sufficient. Jesus names them apostles; they are sent out by Him, authorized by Him, and function under His authority as representatives of His ministry. He tells them, "He who receives you receives me" (Matt. 10:40 NASB). It is He who gives them power and authority over the demons and to heal diseases (Luke 9:1).

Are there *suitable candidates*? As a result of a night of prayer, Jesus calls the twelve whom He specifically chooses. As for preparation, "[t]hey are to be with Him." Their appointment in Luke 6 and their subsequent experiences with Jesus can be seen as a kind of mentoring and development process, so the paradigmatic process is present, but protracted. His calling of Peter, Andrew, James, John, Levi and others is mentioned in some detail in the gospels (Mark 1:16-20; 2:14). They have built and will continue to build a set of experiences with Jesus.[69] Their time with Jesus in his earthly ministry may be seen as a kind of proving ground. Their ultimate appointment is perhaps a post-resurrection event.

Is there a *rite* of ordination here? In the strictest sense the answer is no. There is no mention of the laying on of hands or an anointing with oil. There is a calling apart of the twelve and their return to the multitude in a visible manner. "Jesus came down *with them,* and stood on a level place; and there was a large crowd of His disciples, and a great throng of people" (Luke 6:17 NASB). This event has some similarities to Moses' calling the seventy to himself and accompanying them as they return to the people, so while a specific ceremony may not have been

---

[68] Leon Morris, *Luke*, rev. ed. *Tyndale New Testament Commentaries* (Grand Rapids: Wm. B. Eerdmans, 1988, rpt. 2000), 137.

[69] We will see the importance the church has placed on a period of testing in the development of its pastoral ministers.

involved, Jesus likewise signals His approval as the ultimate
spiritual authority.

The twelve are also given a commission by Jesus at a later
time (Luke 9:1ff.), power and authority to cast out demons and heal
diseases, a command to preach, and specific instruction on how to
carry out their ministry. There is an actual impartation of power
to do miraculous works, as well as to preach the kingdom. Some
commentators assign the ultimate "sending/impartation" to post-
resurrection events, whether the reception of the Holy Spirit (John
20:21), or the Great Commission (Matt. 28:19), or the reception of
power at Pentecost (Acts 1:1ff).

> The disciples were called not only to be with Jesus but also to
> represent him to others. The Gospels hint at this in having the
> disciples sent forth during the ministry (Mark 6:7ff.). Yet the
> definitive sending forth that constituted the apostolate came
> after the resurrection. All the Gospels join the role of the
> disciple to that of the apostle by having the Twelve (or Eleven)
> disciples of the ministry receive the post-resurrectional
> apostolic command (Matt. 28:19; Luke 24: 47-48; John 20:21;
> Marcan Appendix 16:15).[70]

While these events fit into the concept of impartation of
spiritual power and authority, they do not, strictly speaking, meet
the criteria of an ordination in the classic sense. That is perhaps the
point. There is a normalized form for recognition of new ministry,
but not a fixed, unchanging pattern or rite of appointment. Perhaps
an event, regardless of form, which imparts grace for ministry is
sufficient to meet this criterion.

Is there a *congregation* to participate in this process? The
multitude, which is present as Jesus descends from the mount,
includes both disciples and a "great throng." They, as well as the
inhabitants of the villages yet to be evangelized (Luke 9 and 10),

---

[70] Raymond E. Brown, *Priest and Bishop: Biblical Reflections* (New York:
Paulist Press, 1970), 27.

become the congregations of the disciples. For them, the apostles have (and will) become Jesus' deputies, the emissaries of the kingdom. While the six-fold Moses-Joshua model for establishing new leadership is imperfectly kept in this instance, it is still substantially in place.

The Appointment of Matthias

The next event of interest to us is the appointment of Matthias as successor to Judas Iscariot.

> These all with one mind were continually devoting themselves to prayer, along with the women, and Mary the mother of Jesus and with His brothers. And at this time Peter stood up in the midst of the brethren (a gathering of about one hundred and twenty persons was there together), and said, 'Brethren, the scripture had to be fulfilled, which the Holy Spirit foretold by the mouth of David, concerning Judas, who became a guide to those who arrested Jesus. For he was counted among us and received his portion in this ministry . . . For it is written in the book of Psalms, "Let his homestead be made desolate, and let no man dwell in it; and his office let another man take." It is necessary therefore that of the men who have accompanied us all the time that the Lord Jesus went in and out among us ...one of these should become a witness of His resurrection (Acts 1:14-17,20-22 NASB).

They put forward two men, prayed for the Lord to show His will, cast lots, and placed Matthias among the twelve. How does this event measure up to the Moses-Joshua model?

Is this appointment *of the Lord?* Though there are commentators who have doubts about this,[71] it is clear that Peter

---

[71] "Some commentators have argued the recourse to the lot typifies the situation of the church before Pentecost when it did not have the guidance of the Spirit, and others have gone further and claimed that the church acted

sees himself as fulfilling God's requirement, as expressed in
Scripture, for a replacement for Judas. "His office let another take,"
says the Psalm. Prayer is offered for the Lord to make his mind
known concerning which candidate has been chosen "to occupy
this ministry and apostleship from which Judas turned aside to go
to his own place" (Acts 1:25). The disciples surely believed that this
action would only succeed if it was an expression of God's choice
for a twelfth apostle.

Is there a *need* for this ministry? Certainly, in Peter's mind, it
was important to fill Judas's place of apostleship. Jesus had promised
that they would sit on twelve thrones (Matt. 19:28) in the kingdom
at the *parousia*. There was scriptural support for the necessity of
replacing Judas and letting another man take his office (Matt. 19:20).
In the eyes of the 120, there was a need to fill the vacant ministry.
"Luke's purpose was to show that in the apostles the church
possessed reliable guarantors of the truth of its message." [72]

Is there a *suitable candidate*? Peter makes clear the
requirements for consideration. "It is therefore necessary that of
the men who have accompanied us all the time that the Lord Jesus
went in and out among us – beginning with the baptism of John,
until the day that he was taken up from us – one of these should
become a witness of His resurrection" (Acts 1:21-22). Joseph and
Mathias both meet these qualifications. They have a record of
faithfulness and experience. In a word, they are credible candidates
for appointment to office, based on these criteria. Casting of lots as
a method of determining the appropriate candidate is unique here
in the New Testament.

Is a *spiritual authority* involved? Peter is and will be
recognized as the primary leader among the group. Verses 13

wrongly in choosing Matthias; it should have waited for he 'twelfth man' of
God's own choice, Paul, instead of giving God his choice between two others
who are never heard of again." I. Howard Marshall, *The Acts of the Apostles, An
Introduction and Commentary, Tyndale New Testament Commentaries* (Grand
Rapids: William B. Eerdmans Publishing Co., 1980, rpt. 2000), 67.
[72] Marshall, 63.

and 14 mention the presence of the other apostles, along with the female disciples and the Lord's family. They were all present to agree to and participate in the process of selection. There was a *rite* as well. The two men were put forward, prayer was offered, and lots were cast. Matthias was chosen and thereafter numbered with the eleven. Further details as to whether there was an additional rite confirming Matthias' place of ministry are not available.

Matthias is given a specific task – to bear witness of the resurrection – and possibly an impartation of spiritual power. Later in Acts we are told that great power accompanied the ministry of *all* the apostles. "And with great power the apostles were giving witness to the resurrection of the Lord Jesus, and abundant grace was upon them all" (Acts 4:33 NASB). Also, "at the hands of the apostles many signs and wonders were taking place among the people; and they were all with one accord in Solomon's portico. But none of the rest dared to associate with them; however, the people held them in high esteem" (Acts 5:12-13 NASB).

Is there *congregational involvement?* First of all, a congregation of 120 existed, complete with spiritual leadership.[73] We are told that "they" put forward two men, and "they" prayed. It is uncertain who "they" are, but it appears the entire event included the involvement and presence of the 120. Matthias' relationship and status with the 120 changed as a result of his being numbered with the other eleven apostles.

The Ordination of the Seven

The choosing of the seven (Acts 6:1-7) is a New Testament example of establishing new ministers within the church. This event carries most of the marks of our model for ordination. The

---

[73] "The reason for the parenthesis about the number of disciples is that in Jewish law a minimum of 120 Jewish men was required to establish a community with its own council; in Jewish terms the disciples were a body of sufficient size to form a new community." Marshall, 64.

choosing of the seven and placing them in positions of service is a response to the conflict over the "daily serving of food" (Acts 6:1 NASB). Hellenistic widows are overlooked in favor of the Hebraic widows. There is no express statement indicating that the solution (to choose seven men to take charge of the task) is *of the Lord.* The method pursued and the result would lead us to believe that God's favor rested on the decision and process.

The other five elements of ordination are clearly present. There is a *need* – someone to perform the ministry of benevolence.[74] There are *suitable candidates,* "seven men of good reputation, full of the Spirit and of wisdom" (v.3). These men already possess character and a measure of gifting (fullness of the Spirit) to perform this task. *Spiritual authorities* are involved. The apostles are directly responsible for initiating this process, and it is they who lay hands on the seven. There is a *rite* performed – in this case, the laying on of hands by the apostles. Stephen and Philip go on to even more remarkable Spirit-empowered ministries after this event.

Very significant in this passage is the *role of the congregation.* When they are instructed to choose seven, "the statement found approval with the whole congregation; and they chose Stephen . . ." (v.5). It is members of the larger church who make the choice of seven men based on the instructions of the apostles. The congregation brings them before the apostles. A specific concern of the congregation is addressed as a result of this appointment to service. The word of God continues to spread, and the number of disciples increases.

---

[74] Marshall sees the need to maintain peaceful relations in the face of ethnic divisions of the church. "It seems probable that the men appointed were drawn from the Greek-speaking part of the church which had raised the original complaint . . . . The seven names are all Greek, which suggests that their bearers were not Palestinian Jews; it is true that Greek names were used by Palestinian Jews (Andrew, Philip) but apart from Philip, these are unlikely names for Palestinians" (Marshall, 125, 127).

The Missionary Appointment of Paul and Barnabas

Paul and Barnabas go through a kind of commissioning, appointment, or ordination for their mission to plant churches among the diaspora.

> Now there were at Antioch, in the church that was there, prophets and teachers: Barnabas, and Simeon who was called Niger, and Lucius of Cyrene, and Manaen who had been brought up with Herod the tetrarch and Saul. And while they were ministering to the Lord and fasting, the Holy Spirit said, 'Set apart for me Barnabas and Saul for the work to which I have called (*proskeklemai*) them.' Then, when they had fasted and prayed and laid their hands (*epithentes tas cheiras*) on them, they sent them away. So, being sent out by the Holy Spirit, they went down to Seleucia and from there they sailed to Cyprus (Acts 13:1-4 NASB).

This appointment to a special mission is clearly *of the Lord*. The Holy Spirit is seen as the direct author of the process. "Set apart for *me* ... for the work to which *I* have called them" (emphasis mine). There is a *need*. Until now, no purposeful mission to plant churches among the diaspora and the Gentiles has been established, though both the great commission (Matt. 28:19-21) and the promise of the Father (Acts 1:8) call for such a witness.[75]

There are *suitable candidates*. Paul has already heard from the Lord concerning his future ministry (Acts 9:15-16). He spent several years in the Arabian Desert and another unknown period in Tarsus after preaching in Damascus and Jerusalem.

---

[75] "The importance of the present narrative is that it describes the first piece of planned 'overseas mission' carried out by representatives of a particular church, rather than by solitary individuals, and begun by deliberate church decision, inspired by the Spirit, rather than somewhat more causally as a result of persecution." Ibid., 214.

He has ministered for an entire year with the apostolic delegate Barnabas in Antioch. Paul sees himself as having been set apart from his mother's womb as an apostle (Gal. 1:15-16). A remarkable encounter with Christ, a divine call confirmed by Ananias (Acts 9:17), and a period of formation and mentoring with Barnabas has made him ready. His Roman citizenship, linguistic capacities, and cross-cultural savvy make him the right man for the job.

Barnabas, likewise, has a long track record as a generous (Acts 4:36-37), merciful (Acts 9:27), spiritual, and faithful (Acts 11:24) man of God. As a Jew of Cyprus, he likewise has experience in the Hellenistic culture. We can see evidence of the concept of call here. This becomes a very important concept in later literature regarding ordination and Christian ministry. "[T]he work to which I have called (*proskeklemai*) them" (v.2) is significant here. The perfect tense of the verb gives the meaning of an event which began in the past and continues into the present. Thus the calling is an ongoing process in the life of these apostles. It would not be too much to say that the aggregate of their life experience has prepared them for this moment of commissioning and consecration.

Existing *spiritual leadership* is present and involved in the process. The revelation for the consecration of the mission probably comes through one of the listed prophets. They participate in the fasting, prayer, and laying on of hands that constitute the *rite* of ordination. They are in full agreement that this is God's will and purpose and are able to bless the process without reservation. The result of the rite is that they have been "sent out by the Holy Spirit" (v.4). Remarkable spiritual power is witnessed in the ministry of Paul and Barnabas on the missionary journey (Acts 13:11; 14:9-10). While not necessarily a result of the prayer and fasting, it is confirmation of the need for spiritual gifts to carry out the ministry of the Lord.

The *congregation* in Antioch plays a role in this event. It is unclear who is actually present either at the first event when the Holy Spirit spoke, or the second when they are actually prayed over. But it is clear that the congregation in Antioch continues to play a special role in the life and ministry of Paul. He returns there numerous times as the place from which he and Barnabas were commended to the grace of God (Acts 14:26-27; 18:22-23). They are the congregation's apostolic witness to the diaspora, as well as their delegates to the Jerusalem Council (Acts 15:2).

The Prayer over Timothy

Several oft-cited verses relating to ordination are found in I and II Timothy,[76] namely I Tim 1:18; 4:14; 5:22 and II Tim. 1:6. Three of these possibly relate to a single event in Timothy's ministry. The fourth (I Tim. 5:22) we take to relate to the practice of ordination itself.[77] We will take the view that I Tim. 1:18, 4:14, and II Tim 1:6 all address a single event in Timothy's ministry – his ordination, consecration, or setting apart[78] for ministry – either on a local level or, more likely, as an apostolic delegate.

These passages contain some, though not all, of the essential elements of ordination.

Most importantly, there is no direct statement pointing to the idea that Timothy's setting apart is *of God*. It appears from the fact that prophecy accompanies the process (perhaps much like that of Paul and Barnabas) that divine approval is strongly indicated and can be assumed in confirming Timothy in this way. "Timothy, my son, I give you this instruction in keeping with the prophecies once made about you, so that by following them you may fight the good

---

[76] Though the verses in question are not universally recognized as dealing with the ordination of Timothy or even ordination in general.

[77] "An appropriate time span should be allowed (not 'hastily') before laying hands on individuals to set them apart as elders, since this will go a long way toward eliminating the problem [of elder misconduct]." George W. Knight III, *The Pastoral Epistles: A Commentary on the Greek Text* in *New International Greek Testament Commentary* (Grand Rapids: William B. Eerdmans Publishing Co., 1992), 239.

[78] The terminology used here, while important to some, is not germane to the line of reasoning. The reader may choose between the alternate terms, ordain, consecrate, recognize, or set apart, according to tradition or preference.

fight of faith" (I Tim. 1:18 NIV). Such prophecies seemingly point
to divine approval of Timothy's place as a minister of Christ.

There is then the question of *need*. Timothy's entrance into
service on the apostolic team takes place early in Paul's second
missionary journey. "[Paul] came to Derbe and Lystra, where
a disciple named Timothy lived . . . The brothers at Lystra and
Iconium spoke well of him. Paul wanted to take him along on the
journey" (Acts 16:1,3a NIV). Only a short while before, Paul and
Barnabas had fallen into grave dissension about the choice of co-
workers for the journey. After refusing John Mark and parting
from Barnabas, Paul chooses Silas. Only a short time later he adds
Timothy to the team, filling the need for an assistant on the second
apostolic mission. As Paul's church planting ministry expands,
Timothy comes to take a primary role as an apostolic delegate. This
setting apart is most likely related to that ministry calling. In such
a case it would closely mirror Paul's consecration as a missionary
to the diaspora (Acts 13:1-4).

There is no doubt of Paul's need for assistance in overseeing
his far-flung mission, and Timothy's worth is proven. "I hope in the
Lord Jesus to send Timothy to you soon, that I also may be cheered
when I receive news about you. I have no one else like him, who
will show genuine concern for your welfare" (Phil. 2:19 NIV).
After his separation from the Thessalonian church, he depends on
his co-worker: "So when we could stand it no longer, we thought it
best to be left by ourselves in Athens. We sent Timothy, who is our
brother and God's fellow worker in spreading the gospel of Christ,
to strengthen and encourage you in your faith . . ." (I Thess. 3:1-2
NIV). Timothy's ministry fills a proven *need*.

The issue of a *suitable candidate* to fill the need for an
apostolic assistant is also addressed by the previous citations. It is
unclear exactly when Timothy's ordination takes place, whether
early or later in his relationship with Paul. It is clear that Timothy
has the recommendation of the believers in Galatia; they spoke
well of him. No mention is made of a consecration service at this
time, though Timothy, because of his mixed-Jewish background,

is circumcised (Acts 16:3). The laying on of hands may have
taken place much later. If so, then Timothy's ministry would have
undergone an extended and, given the nature of Paul's ministry,
intensive period of mentoring and development. Normally we
would look for this extended proving period before ordination. In
fact, Paul's admonition to Timothy[79] against recognizing a novice
(neophutos; I Tim. 3:6) as an overseer would indicate that the rite
took place later in Timothy's development rather than sooner.

The issue of the endorsement of *existing spiritual authorities*
is a given in context. Paul exhorts, "For this reason I remind you to
fan into flame the gift of God which is in you through the laying
on of my hands" (II Tim. 1:6), and again, "Do not neglect your
gift, which was given you through a prophetic message when the
body of elders laid their hands on you" (I Tim. 4:14). The brothers
in Lystra had commended Timothy. Paul himself and a presbytery
from an undesignated place also participated in blessing Timothy's
ministry through the laying on of hands.

A *rite,* including the laying on of hands and prophetic
utterance, is also a given in context. The rite includes an
impartation of divine power, a spiritual gift to be used in the
fulfillment of Timothy's ministry. This closely parallels the
Moses-Joshua paradigm of imparted wisdom. The laying on of
hands accompanied by prophetic speech is a means of imparting
spiritual power to Timothy. This is perhaps similar to the blessing
of Jacob by Isaac.[80] His blessing also contained words of prophetic
significance. "Isaac trembled violently and said, 'Who was it, then,
that hunted game and brought it to me? I ate it just before you came

---

[79] Pauline authorship of Timothy and Titus is assumed here.

[80] "The basic idea in early Christian ordination was not creating a substitute
or transferring authority, but conferring a blessing and petitioning for the
divine favor. Blessing, of course, in ancient thought was more than a kindly
wish; it was thought as imparting something very definite (as in the patriarchal
blessings of the Old Testament)" Everett Ferguson, "Laying on of Hands: Its
Significance in Ordination" *The Journal of Theological Studies,* April, 1975,
Vol. XXVI, Part 1, p. 2.

and I blessed him – and indeed he will be blessed…I have made him lord over you and have made all his relatives his servants, and I have sustained him with grain and new wine'" (27:33,37 NIV). Isaac recognized that the blessing unwittingly given could not be revoked – "indeed he will be blessed." Similarly, Jacob realized the power of his words when blessing Joseph's children with the laying on of hands, declaring with his right hand that Ephraim's descendants would be greater than Manasseh's (Gen. 48:17-20). In the same way, Timothy's ordination was marked by an impartation of spiritual power.

The *presence of a congregation* in Timothy's case is unclear. The fact that he served many congregations as Paul's surrogate is indisputable. He is urged to fulfill his public ministry as a result of his ordination. "Until I come, devote yourself to the public reading of Scripture, to preaching and to teaching" (I Tim. 4:13 NIV). Our knowledge of the congregational role in choosing Timothy is limited to the initial recommendation (Acts 16:2). A statement of Paul's, "Do not let anyone look down on you because you are young" (I Tim. 4:12 NIV), indicates that relations with the churches may have been difficult because of his youth. He is encouraged to remember his ordination and use the gift he had received at that time.

In another verse Paul warns against misusing the laying on of hands. "Do not be hasty in the laying on of hands, and do not share in the sins of others" (I Tim. 5:22 NIV). This comment refers to ordination, restoring a fallen elder, or restoring a penitent.[81] A traditional view of this verse warns against hasty ordinations, which violate the essential elements of a proper confirmation of candidates for presbyter.[82]

---

[81] There are many discussions in the literature about the meaning of this verse and its significance for our purposes. For instance see Warkentin, 144-152.

[82] As in Gordon Fee, *1 and 2 Timothy, Titus* in *New International Biblical Commentary* (Peabody, MA: Hendrickson Publishers, 1984), 131. "The point of this imperative is as in 3:6, that Timothy must exercise proper caution before laying hands on people to be recognized as elders (cf. 4:14). The reason for

Two other passages in the pastorals are significant for our purposes. They are parallel in content. I Tim. 3:1-13 deals with recognition of overseers and deacons, and Titus 1: 5-9 speaks to the appointment of elders or overseers. The qualifications for office address the question of suitable candidates. In our previous examples, the questions of character and suitability are limited to "having the Spirit" (Num. 27:18), or being full of the spirit and wisdom (Acts 6:3), or meeting the requirements of experience (Matthias in Acts 1:21), or having a good recommendation (Acts 16:2). Of course, all of these relate to character and aptitude.

The pastorals are extensive in their recommendations and will serve as a pattern for the post-apostolic church.[83] Qualities such as desire for the work; blamelessness of reputation; freedom from debilitating vices such as anger, addictions, marital infidelity, and greed; capable management of the home; ability to teach; an irenic spirit; and experience in the faith (i.e. not being a neophyte) are critical to candidate selection in the pastorals. These requirements emerge significantly in the post-apostolic church as we further examine essential elements of recognition, nurture and confirmation of candidates for ministry positions in the church.

---

caution has to do with sin, that is, the fact that some are now sinning (v. 20) and that not all people's sins are readily apparent (v. 24)."
[83] For instance, the *Apostolic Constitutions.*

Chapter Four
Patterns of Ordination in Scripture:
Paradigm Breakers

Thus far we have established a general biblical pattern
for recognizing and setting apart spiritual leaders. Its elements
can be narrowed down to the six essentials: 1) divine initiative;
2) congregational or ministry need; 3) suitable candidate; 4)
participation of spiritual authorities; 5) a rite of ordination or
consecration with impartation of spiritual power; and 6) the role of
and subsequent change in relationship with the congregation. It is
also clear that this pattern varies. Segments are sometimes delayed,
or even omitted altogether.

There are some cases in Scripture where several elements
are omitted and the pattern is obscured or missing. The situation
of Amos the prophet was mentioned in the first chapter. Spiritual
authorities and rite are entirely omitted in his case, yet the legitimacy
of Amos' prophetic ministry is unquestioned. Also, Moses' calling
was surely "of the Lord," but was not mediated by any human
agency or rite. There are other exceptions, or paradigm breakers, as
well. These examples make it clear that the elements of ordination
identified above cannot be considered a requirement for ministry.

Elijah and Elisha

Elijah the prophet simply appears on the scene in I Kings
17. We are told little about his background and nothing of his
spiritual formation. To our knowledge, no spiritual authority has

acknowledged him. He relates to no congregation;[84] he has received
no ritual confirmation of his ministry role. Yet the power and
impact of his ministry, and the need for his prophetic gift in a time
of apostasy in the Northern Kingdom are indisputable.

It is Elijah's recognition of Elisha that serves as our paradigm
breaker. After a great victory over the prophets of Baal at Carmel
and an extended fast, the Lord instructs Elijah, "Elisha the son
of Shaphat of Abel-meholah you shall anoint as prophet in your
place" (I Kings 19:16 NASB). When Elijah encounters Elisha, a
very simple act serves to separate Elisha from his daily activities to
follow Elijah:

> So he departed there and found Elisha the son of Shaphat,
> while he was plowing with twelve pairs of oxen before him,
> and he with the twelfth. And Elijah passed over to him and
> threw his mantle on him. And he left the oxen and ran after
> Elijah and said 'Please let me kiss my father and my mother,
> then I will follow you.' And he said to him, 'Go back again,
> for what have I done to you?' (I Kings 19:19-20 NASB).

After feasting with his family and neighbors, "Then he
arose and followed Elijah and ministered to him" (I Kings 19:21).
Later, when Elijah is taken up, his mantle falls to Elisha, there is an
impartation of power, and the people recognize Elisha's authority
because of the miracles he performs.

Elisha's recognition does not take the conventional liturgical
forms. His consecration as a leader is *of the Lord*, for his choice
as prophet is revealed to Elijah by the word of the Lord. There is
a *need* for Elisha's ministry of prophetic leadership once Elijah
departs the scene. Elijah not only chose Elisha as *the candidate* to

---

[84] At one point he laments the fact that he is very alone. "He said, 'I have
been very jealous for the Lord, the God of hosts. For the people of Israel have
forsaken your covenant, thrown down your altars, and killed your prophets with
the sword, and I, even I only, am left, and they seek my life to take it away'"(I
Kings 19:10 ESV).

be his successor, but he mentored him through close contact – "he followed Elijah and ministered to him." He is recognized as one "who used to poured water on the hands of Elijah" (II Kings 3:11). Elijah, of course, serves as *the spiritual authority* in the choice of Elisha as his successor.

While Elijah had been told to anoint Elisha, there is no discussion of such a ritual anointing. The *rite* seems to be wrapped up (pun intended) in Elijah's cloak, both the initial call to follow and the actual reception of Elijah's prophetic ministry. Thus we speak today of receiving someone's mantle. Elijah "threw his mantle on him" and "[h]e then took up Elijah's prophet's mantle, which had fallen from him when he was snatched away, and returned to the Jordan." The master's prophetic mantle fell to Elisha as Elijah was taken up, as a pledge to Elisha "that his request was fulfilled, *and as a visible sign to others that he was the divinely appointed successor, and that the spirit of Elijah rested on him* (emphasis mine)." [85]

In this case, the rite of passing on the mantle includes a tremendous impartation of spiritual power:

> He also took up the mantle that fell from him, and returned and stood by the bank of the Jordan. And he took the mantle of Elijah that fell from him, and struck the waters and said, 'Where is the Lord, the God of Elijah?' And when he also had struck the waters, they were divided here and there; and Elijah crossed over. Now the sons of the prophets who were at Jericho opposite him saw him, they said, 'The spirit of Elijah rests on Elisha. And they came to meet him and bowed themselves to the ground before him (II Kings 2:13-15 NASB).

---

[85] Keil and Delitzsch, *Old Testament Commentaries*, vol. 2 (Grand Rapids: Associated Authors and Publishers, Inc.), 750.

The *congregation*, the sons of the prophets, immediately recognize Elisha's authority and bow in respect to him. Their relationship has been transformed.

Though the essential elements of ordination exist in the Elijah- Elisha relationship, it would be uncommon for anyone to refer to this as an ordination. Nevertheless, it performs precisely the same function – to recognize and establish spiritual authority. This is precisely the point. Spiritual calling and fruitful ministry may or may not be affirmed by a rite of ordination. Recognition itself may take different forms. Yet in some fashion, the essential elements of ordination are at least partially present in the exercise of true ministry.

John the Baptist

Another paradigm breaker is John the Baptist. His birth is miraculous. From the womb, it is clear he will be a prophet of God. "And you, child, will be called the prophet of the Most High; for you will go before the Lord to prepare his ways, to give knowledge of salvation to his people in the forgiveness of their sins, because of the tender mercy of our God"(Luke 1:76-78 ESV). Through this prophecy, we see John's ministry is *of the Lord.* There is a *need,* perhaps as yet unrecognized, for one to prepare the way of the Christ.

As a *candidate*, John clearly possesses a call from God, and through growth and preparation becomes ready for his ministry. "And the child grew and became strong in spirit, and he was in the wilderness until the day of his public appearance to Israel" (Luke 1:80 ESV). There is no mention of *spiritual authorities* or a *rite* for John. This is where he breaks precedent in terms of the elements of ordination. While the apparent spiritual authorities are curious about his ministry (Matt. 3:7; John 1:19 ff.), they do not validate it. In fact, they "did not believe him" (Matt. 21:25 ESV; also see 21:32).

This is the crux. In this case, the concept of essential elements of ordination breaks down on the issue of human recognition. While the recognition and ritual blessing of a candidate by spiritual authorities is a general pattern in the Bible, it is sometimes entirely bypassed or rejected. John the Baptist is a prime example. The ultimate example is Jesus the Messiah.

By what authority?

Jesus' interaction with the religious establishment of His day was marked by conflict, rejection, and ultimately death on the cross. The conflict over His ministry in the temple revolved around His right or credentials for ministry. After cleansing the temple, He is asked, "By what authority are you doing these things and who gave you that authority?"(Matt. 21:23 ESV).

Of course, Jesus' ministry was *of God.* The gospel accounts repeatedly refer to his election by God and establish the miraculous nature of his birth (Matt. 1:18-2:12; Luke 1:26-38; 2:1-38). Much post-resurrection preaching focuses not only on the signs surrounding his birth, but on the fulfillment of Old Testament prophecy, as in Matthew's gospel. The coming of the Messiah was the recognized *need* and even longing of people such as Simeon and Anna (Luke 2: 25-38).

When confronted about his credentials for ministry, Jesus did make references which take us back to the essentials. Humanly speaking, Jesus' baptism by John, and the opening of the heavens was the means of His recognition by spiritual authority and a rite of consecration, without human hands.

> And when Jesus was baptized, immediately he went up from the water, and behold, the heavens were opened to him, and he saw the Spirit of God descending like a dove and coming to rest on him; and behold a voice from heaven said, 'This is my beloved Son, with whom I am well pleased.' (Matthew 3:16-17 ESV).

Immediately after His baptism He was led into the wilderness by the Spirit, and afterward began His public ministry.

The duly ordained Sanhedrin members[86] seemed unaware of the fact that it is only *in the Lord* and *of the Lord* that ministry has any legitimacy at all. This leads Jesus to ask the central question, "Was John's baptism from heaven or from men?" (Matt. 21:25). Consequently, due to their ignorance, and inability to answer this question, it was their lot that the vineyard would be taken from them and given to others who would bear its fruit (Matt. 21:43).

Summary thoughts on paradigm breakers

So we see from these many examples that a pattern of essential elements of ordination exists for various forms of spiritual leadership in both the Old and New Testaments. Sometimes the pattern is altered, and some of the elements even eliminated. Sometimes, as in the case of John the Baptist and Jesus, recognition by spiritual authorities or a visible ordination rite is entirely missing. This, of course, does not eliminate the legitimacy of the ministry, nor does it detract from the validity of the concept of essential elements of ordination.

---

[86] J.Z. Lauterbauch, 'Ordination," *The Jewish Encyclopedia,* Vol. IX (New York: Funk and Wagnall, 1905), 428.

Chapter Five
The Essential Elements of
Ordination in Church History

Is there evidence of this six-fold pattern in ordination practices throughout church history? If so, it is probably not consciously observed. The question is: Has the church universally recognized across time and denomination certain elements essential to the process of ordination? It is my contention that the churches have tended to follow a pattern of essential elements in recognizing, cultivating, and confirming their spiritual leaders. We will use a limited number of examples from the documents of church history to identify whether these six essential elements characterize the process of ordination.

First Element: Is the Ordination of God?

Has the church always recognized that ordination is a process initiated and confirmed by God Himself, that it is not a matter of simply human choice or invention? In the New Testament, several passages emphasize the Lord's role in distributing spiritual gifts. "All these are the work of one and the same Spirit, and he gives them to each one, *just as he determines*" (I Cor. 12:1, NIV, emphasis mine). Also, "*It was he who gave* some to be apostles, some to be prophets, some to be evangelists, and some to be pastors and teachers" (Eph. 4:11, NIV, emphasis mine). Or, even more to the point, "Keep watch over yourselves and all the flock of which *the Holy Spirit has made you* overseers" (Acts 20:28

NIV, emphasis mine). Here we see that the Spirit's distribution of gifts is the determining factor in establishing ministries in the church.

In Clement's epistle to the Corinthians (*c.* 95), chapters forty through forty-four repeatedly indicate that the ministry is established by God through Christ and His apostles and, because of its divine origin, is worthy of obedience and respect.

Ignatius, in his letter to the Philadelphians (*c.* 107), praises their bishop as one who "was not selected to undertake the ministry which pertains to the common[weal], either by himself, or out of vainglory, but by the love of Jesus Christ, and of God the Father . . . ."[87]

The earliest ordination prayer from the Apostolic Tradition of Hippolytus (*c.* 217) emphasizes the role of God as the one who chooses the episcopal candidate and who initiates the ordination process.

> God and Father of our Lord Jesus Christ . . . *establishing princes and priests and not leaving thy sanctuary without a ministry,* thou since the beginning of the world hast had pleasure among those whom thou hast chosen to be given . . . . Father who knowest the heart, grant to this thy servant *whom thou hast chosen* for a bishopric, to feed thy flock . . . . (emphasis mine)[88]

Geoffrey Wainwright points out, "In the sacramentaries, the Roman prayers at the ordination of bishops, presbyters, and deacons begin . . . 'assist us, we beseech thee, almighty God, giver of honors, *distributer of orders, and bestower of offices* . . . .'" (emphasis mine).[89]

---

[87] "The Epistle of Ignatius to the Philadelphians" in *Ante-Nicene Fathers*, vol. 1, Alexander Roberts and James Donaldson, eds., 79.
[88] Geoffrey Wainwright, "Some Theological Aspects of Ordination" in *Ordination Rites Past and Present p. 125-126.*
[89] Ibid., 130-131.

Cyprian affirms in several places that appointment to office is "of God." For instance, in reference to the ordination of a young man named Aurelius, "In ordination of the clergy, brethren, we usually consult you [the congregation] beforehand and weigh the character and deserts of individuals, with the general counsel [of all]. However, human testimonies must not be waited for when the divine approval comes first." [90] Or again, "Cornelius was made bishop *by the judgment of God and His Christ*, by the testimony of almost all of the clergy, by the election of the people who were then present, and by the assembly of ancient priests and good men" (emphasis mine). [91]

A section of the Apostolic Constitutions (*c.* 390) states the principle in this way:

> Not everyone who wants to [be] is ordained – as was the case with that counterfeit priesthood of the calves under Jeroboam. Rather, *only he who is called of God* is ordained . . . . We are only saying that no one snatches the priestly dignity to himself. He either receives it from God – as did Melchizedek and Job – or from a high priest – as did Aaron from Moses. Now Philip and Ananias did not ordain themselves, but were appointed by Christ, the High Priest (emphasis mine).[92]

Chrysostom, in his classic "Treatise Concerning the Christian Priesthood," covers all six of the essential elements

---

[90] Cyprian 5.312, in "Ordination" in *A Dictionary of Early Christian Beliefs*, David W. Bercot, ed. (Peabody, MA: Hendrickson Publishers, Inc, 1998). Note also the reference to congregational input.
[91] Ibid., Cyprian, 5. 329. Note again reference to testimony from existing clergy and congregational affirmation.
[92] Apostolic Constitutions, 7.499, 500 in "Ordination," *A Dictionary of Early Christian Beliefs.* There is a reference in this passage to Philip and Ananias because they performed what was considered by the time of the Apostolic Constitutions (*c.* 390) to be the "priestly duty" of baptism. They seem self-ordained in this context, but this is not the point of the discussion in the Constitutions.

related to ordination. Regarding the role of God in choosing candidates for ordination through the Holy Spirit, he states, "For the priestly office is indeed discharged on earth, but it ranks among the heavenly ordinances . . . but *the Paraclete Himself, instituted this vocation*, and persuaded men while still abiding in the flesh to represent the ministry of angels"(emphasis mine). [93] And speaking of the heavenly source of the priestly authority, he writes, "For they who inhabit the earth and make their abode there are entrusted with the administration of things which are in Heaven, and have received an authority which God has not given to angels or archangels."[94]

In his discussion of King Saul's failures, Chrysostom makes clear that his position of leadership was the gift of God. "For he who has been promoted to great honor by God, must not advance the greatness of his honor as an excuse for his errors, but should make God's special favor towards him the motive for further improvement . . . ."[95] He thus shows that even the Old Testament kingship is bestowed through the favor of God.

In a discussion of those who are called against their will, he contrasts those who grasp position with those who are called, writing that "many of the ordinations now-a-days do not proceed from the grace of God, but are due to human ambition." [96] At the end of his treatise he assures his friend Basil that it is Christ who has called him and set him over his own flock.[97]

Calvin addresses the question of sovereign appointment of ministers through the concept of call.

> Wherefore, lest restless and turbulent men should presumptuously push themselves forward to teach or rule . . .

---

[93] John Chrysostom, "On the Priesthood," III,4 in NPNF, Vol. 9, First Series, Philip Schaff, ed. p, 46.
[94] Ibid., III,5, 47.
[95] Ibid., IV, 1, 61
[96] Ibid., IV, 1, 61
[97] Ibid., VI, 13, 83.

it was expressly provided that no one should assume a public office in the Church without a call (Heb. 5:4; Jer. 17:16). Therefore, if any one would be deemed a true minister of the Church, he must *first* be duly called; and, *secondly*, he must answer to his calling; that is, undertake and execute the office assigned to him. This may often be observed in Paul, who, when he would approve his apostleship, almost always alleges a call . . . . If so great a minister of Christ dares not arrogate to himself authority to be heard in the Church, *unless as having been appointed to it by the command of the Lord*, and faithfully performing what has been entrusted to him, how great the effrontery for any man, devoid of one or both of them, to demand for himself such honor (emphasis mine).[98]

And speaking of the Lord's hand in choosing the minister, Calvin further states, "For those whom the Lord destined for this great office he previously provides with the armor which is requisite for the discharge of it . . . ."[99] Calvin goes on to say that "no one could duly perform the office unless called by God." [100]

God's role in establishing church officers is noted in the Puritan Cambridge Platform (1648). "No man may take the honor of a church officer unto himself, but he that was called of God, as was Aaron."[101] The Savoy Platform (1658) was a statement of those English Puritans who favored Independent as opposed to Presbyterian church government. They were careful to clarify that church officers were to be appointed in the manner of Christ's choosing, again demonstrating the divine role in the process of ordination. "The way appointed by Christ for the calling of any persons, *fitted and gifted by the Holy Ghost,* unto the office of pastor, teacher or elder in a church is, that he be chosen thereunto

---

[98] John Calvin, *Institutes of the Christian Religion*, IV, iii, 10.

[99] Ibid., IV, iii, 11, 567.

[100] Ibid., IV, iii, 13, 568.

[101] The Cambridge Platform, in *The Reformation of the Church,* 252.

by the common suffrage of the church itself" (emphasis mine).[102]
The platform goes on to say, "A church furnished with officers
(*according to the mind of Christ*) hath full power to administer all
his ordinances" (emphasis mine).[103]

The Savoy Platform, in opposition to clericalism, goes so
far as to say, "Ordination alone without election or precedent
consent of the church, by those who formerly have been ordained
by virtue of the power they have received by their ordination,
doth not constitute any person a church officer, or communicate
office power unto him."[104] This statement emphasizes Reformed
insistence on congregational suffrage as a means of validating an
ordinand along with the belief that ordination must be performed
according to this divine pattern.

Richard Baxter, in *The Reformed Pastor,* makes Christ's
preeminence in the selection process clear: "By a pastor or a bishop
is here meant an officer *appointed by Christ* for the ordinary
teaching and guiding of a particular church and all its members, in
order that they may be saved and walk in a way that is pleasing to
God" (emphasis mine).[105]

One of the strongest statements in favor of the sufficiency
of only a personal call of God to the ministry is the Quaker
declaration *Theses Theologicae* of Robert Barclay (1675).
According to Barclay it is this inner light of personal call which
establishes the ministry:

> [A]nd by the leading, moving, and drawing hereof ought every
> evangelist and Christian pastor be led and ordered in his labor
> and work of the gospel, both as to the place where, as to the
> persons to whom, and as to the times when he is to minister.
> Moreover, those who have this authority may and ought to

---

[102] The Savoy Platform 1658 in *The Reformation of the Church,* 277.
[103] Ibid., 278.
[104] Ibid., p. 278.
[105] Richard Baxter, *The Reformed Pastor.* (Marshallton, DE: The National Foundation for Christian Education, n.d.), 2.

preach the gospel, though without human commission or literature; as, on the other hand, those who want [i.e. lack] the authority of this divine gift, however learned or authorized by the commissions of men and churches, are to be esteemed but as deceivers, and not true ministers of the gospel.[106]

Clearly, for Barclay and the early Quakers, an outward rite or commission was both unnecessary and possibly even detrimental.

In the later Catholic system, the documents of Vatican II recognize the role of the Holy Spirit in establishing bishops in the church, albeit under the leadership of the Bishop of Rome. "The bishops have also been designated *by the Holy Spirit* to take the place of the apostles as pastors of souls and, together with the Supreme Pontiff and subject to his authority, they are commissioned to perpetuate the work of Christ, the eternal Pastor" (emphasis mine).[107]

The 1994 *Catechism of the Catholic Church* further confirms the historic belief in the divine origin of a call to public ministry (in this case priesthood) in the church.

> No one has a *right* to receive the sacrament of Holy Orders. Indeed, no one claims this office for himself. He is called to it by God. Anyone who thinks he recognizes the signs of God's call to the ordained ministry must humbly submit his desire to the authority of the Church . . . . Like every grace this sacrament can be *received* only as an unmerited gift.[108]

Though this passage emphasizes the mediatorial role of the believing community, *i.e.* the Church in communion with the

---

[106] Robert Barcaly, "Theses Theologicae," in *Creeds of the Churches,* Leith, 330.

[107] "Decree on the Pastoral Office of Bishops in the Church," *Vatican Council II, The Conciliar and Post Conciliar Documents. (*Colegeville, MN: Liturgical Press, 1975), 555.

[108] *Catechism of the Catholic Church.* (New York: Doubleday, 1994), 440, entry 1578.

bishop, it nevertheless adheres to the traditional belief that grace for ministry is conferred by God himself and is not a result of self-appointment. Note the similarities in the matter of community participation in the selection process with the Savoy Platform as quoted above. We will explore this further under the last heading, the role of the congregation.

Second Element: Is a Specific Need Addressed by the Ministry?

Has appointment to a specific ministry within the believing community been critical to the church's decisions about ordination in the past? Has an "at-large" ordination that makes an individual a universal cleric been the norm in the practice of the church historically? Have all churches taken this or another approach?

Within the post-apostolic literature, the *Didache* first discusses the settled role of bishops and deacons juxtaposed with traveling prophets and teachers.

> Appoint for yourselves therefore bishops and deacons worthy of the Lord, men who are meek and not lovers of money, and true and approved; for unto you they also perform the service of prophets and teachers. Therefore despise them not; for they are your honorable men along with the prophets and teachers.[109]

This concept of a settled ministry becomes the primary system of church order in the period of the Apostolic Fathers. A three-tiered order of bishop, presbyter, and deacon with specific duties emerges after the time of Ignatius of Antioch.[110]

---

[109] J.B. Lightfoot, ed. "The Teaching of the Lord to the Gentiles by the Twelve Apostle," xv, in *The Apostolic Fathers*. (1891 rpt., Grand Rapids; Baker Book House, 1956), 128

[110] The early, broad establishment of the three-tiered order of ministry is by no means universally accepted by patristic scholars. An early modern discussion

The traveling ministries of prophet and teacher disappear in the literature. Archbishops and metropolitans eventually take on the role of apostolic oversight within specific bounds.

In fact, by the time of Nicaea a canon appears prohibiting peripatetic ministries. "Neither bishop, presbyter, nor deacon shall pass from city to city, but they shall be sent back should they attempt to do so, to the Churches in which they were ordained" (Ancient Epitome of Cannon XV, Nicaea).[111] Canon XVI reinforces this prohibition.

> Such presbyters or deacons as desert their own Church are not to be admitted into another, but are to be sent back to their own diocese. But if any bishop should ordain one who belongs to another Church without the consent of his own bishop, the ordination shall be cancelled (Ancient Epitome of Canon XVI, Nicaea). [112]

Additional boundaries for metropolitan bishops were defined by Canons VI and VII, thus establishing the clear concept of episcopal role and jurisdiction in a legal sense for the patristic church.

In the century before Nicaea, Origen, the famous un-ordained scholar-teacher at the Catechetical School in Alexandria, stirred great controversy by receiving an unauthorized ordination on a trip through Palestine at Caesarea. According to Eusebius, "The matters that were agitated concerning him on this account, and the decisions on these matters by those who presided over the churches . . . demand a separate treatise."[113]

This incident simply shows that even early on, the concept

---

of the question is found in Robert Ellis Thompson, *The Historic Episcopate* (Philadelphia: Westminster Press, 1910). The later patristic church came to recognize seven orders (Rome) and the Eastern Churches five orders. For a brief discussion, Alton McEachern, *Set Apart for Service*, 34, 36.
[111] *The Seven Ecumenical Councils,* NPNF, Second series, vol. 14, 32.
[112] Ibid., 35. Canon XVIII addresses similar behavior in deacons in an effort to fix the bounds of diaconal ministry.
[113] *The Church History of Eusebius* VI, 24 in NPNF Second Series, vol. 1.p.271.

of ordination carried the idea of a specific charge or ministry that was not necessarily transferable to other geographical regions or churches. That is, ordination to the priesthood or diaconate was need-specific. Even a bishop was not permitted to claim dominion beyond defined boundaries.[114] Ordination was not "at-large."

Noted theologian-bishop Gregory Nazianzen fell into difficulties on this very account:

> The general feeling, however, of the early Church was certainly very strong against all changes of Episcopal cure, and there can be no doubt that the chief reason why St. Gregory Nazianzen resigned the Presidency of the First Council of Constantinople, was because he had been translated from his obscure see Sasima . . . to the Imperial City.[115]

That resignation is poignantly recorded in his Oration LXII, "The Last Farewell," given at the Council of Constantinople. [116]

---

[114] This does not preclude the then looming conflicts over the established jurisdiction of the Metropolitans and particularly that of the Bishop of Rome, whose claim to universal jurisdiction has been the source of schism, conflict, and theological rupture in the church through the centuries.

[115] "Excursus on the Translation of Bishops," in *The Seven Ecumenical Councils,* NPNF, Second Series, vol. 14, p. 33. This excursus also notes that, "The grounds on which prohibition rested were usually that such changes were the outcome of ambition, and that if tolerated the result would be that smaller and less important sees would be despised, and that here would be a constant temptation for the bishops of such sees to make themselves popular with the important persons in other dioceses with the hope of promotion."

[116] Gregory Nazianzen, "Oration LXII, The Last Farewell," in NPNF, Second Series, vol. 7, 392. This sermon is a most poignant account of Gregory's many years of labor in Constantinople and the remarkable outcome of his ministry there. "You have now, my friends, heard the defense of my presence here: if it be deserving of praise thanks are due for it to God, and to you who called me; if it has fallen below your expectation, I give thanks even on this behalf. For I am assured that it has not been altogether deserving of censure, and am confident that you also admit this. Have we made at all a gain of this people? Have we consulted at all our own interests, as I see is most often the case? Have we caused any vexation to the Church? . . . . Give me a respite from my long

A successor of Gregory's, John Chrysostom, in his "Treatise Concerning the Christian Priesthood" addresses the specific nature and purpose to which the minister is called. "[H]e who is entrusted with its [*i.e.* the church's] care ought to train it up to a state of healthiness, and beauty unspeakable, and to look everywhere, lest any spot or wrinkle, or other like blemish should mar its vigor and comeliness."[117]

The Eastern Orthodox rejected the concept of absolute ordination, or ordination at-large. According to McEachern, the Church of Rome began to view ordination differently around the year 1200. With the bestowal of special powers (to pray over the Eucharist) and a special character came an "absolute ordination." The Orthodox had stated in 1140, "We decree that no person ought to be ordained in an absolute manner, neither priest, nor deacon, nor any cleric."[118] On the contrary, the Roman Catholic Council of Trent in 1563 stated that sacramental character was conferred at ordination.[119]

Later, Martin Luther clarifies the role of the ordained minister within the flock, giving it a very clear definition. As cited in the introduction, Luther assigned the bounds of the ministry very specifically to administration of word and sacrament.

> [W]e all have the same authority in regard to the word and the sacraments, although no one has the right to administer them without the consent of the members of his church, or by the call of the majority (because when something is common to

---

labors; give honor to my foreign service; elect another in my place, the one who is being eagerly sought on your behalf, someone who is able to gratify you on all points, and share with you the ecclesiastical cares."

[117] John Chrysostom, "On the Priesthood," IV, 2, NPNF, First Series, vol. 9, 65. In Book II, 2 he emphasizes that the primary role of the minister/priest is specifically to care for the flock of Christ. A sentiment to be echoed later by Calvin.

[118] McEachern, *Set Apart for Service*, 35-36.

[119] Ibid., 37

all, no single person is empowered to arrogate it to himself, but should await the call of the church).[120]

And Calvin speaks to the issue of specific need, or sphere of ministry, pointedly in the *Institutes*:

But herein they most shamefully corrupt the ancient institution that they by their ordination appoint not presbyters to guide and feed the people, but priests to sacrifice. In like manner, when they consecrate deacons, they pay no regard to their true and proper office, but only ordain to certain ceremonies concerning the cup and paten. But in the Council of Chalcedon it was, on the contrary, decreed that there should be no absolute ordinations, that is, ordinations without assigning to the ordained a place where they were to exercise their office . . . .

[I]s it not at all times absurd to appoint a presbyter without assigning him a locality? For when they ordain it is only to sacrifice. But the legitimate ordination of a presbyter is to the Government of the Church, while deacons are called to the charge of alms.[121]

Calvin is also concerned, as were the Canons of Nicaea, with the self-transfer of pastors and their tendency to mind matters not assigned to them. In this way the Reformer affirms that appointment to ministry involves a specific place and service to the specific needs of a given segment of Christ's flock.

While we assign a church to each pastor, we deny not that he who is affixed to one church may assist other churches,

---

[120] Martin Luther, "Pagan Servitude of the Church," in *Martin Luther, Selections from His Writings,* John Dillenberger, ed. (Garden city, NY: Anchor Books, 1961), 349.
[121] *Institutes*, IV,v, 4,5, 580.

whether any disturbance has occurred which requires his presence, or his advice is asked on some doubtful matter. But because that policy is necessary to maintain the peace of the Church, each has his proper duty assigned, lest all should become disorderly, run up and down without any certain vocation, flock together promiscuously to one spot, and capriciously leave the churches vacant, being more solicitous for their own convenience than for the edification of the Church. This arrangement aught, as far as possible, to be commonly observed, that every one, content with his own limits, may not encroach on another's province.[122]

Likewise, Article XXIII of the Thirty-Nine Articles of the Anglican Church addresses the purpose of ordination and the specific need which is being filled.

It is not lawful for any man to take upon him the office of public preaching, or ministering the Sacraments in the Congregation, before he be lawfully called and sent to execute the same.[123]

The Cambridge Platform (1648), the American counterpart to the Westminster Confession of Faith, was adopted by the New England church and civil government in 1651. Among other things it addressed issues of church government, particularly the Congregational concept of elder ordination to a specific charge.

[E]lders being appointed to feed, not all flocks, but the particular flock of God over which the Holy Ghost had made them overseers, and that flock they must attend, even the whole flock; and one congregation being as much as any ordinary elders can attend, therefore there is no greater

---

[122] *Institutes*, IV, iii, 7, 565.
[123] Leith, 274.

church than a congregation, which may ordinarily meet in one place.[124]

The Cambridge Platform also speaks to the issue of "at-large" ministries, clarifying that ministry is need-based, not title-based. The Platform recommends a kind of re-ordination when a call is extended by a second congregation to a minister or elder who departs a previous charge.[125]

> He that is clearly loosed from his office-relation unto that church whereof he was a minister, cannot be looked at as an officer, nor perform any act of office in any other church, unless he be again orderly called unto office: which when it shall be, we know nothing to hinder, but imposition of hands also in his ordination ought to be used towards him again. For so Paul the apostle received imposition of hands twice at least, from Ananias, Acts 9:17 and Acts 13:3.[126]

Another issue relating to the purpose of ministry was the question of order. Did local congregations need oversight from trans-local authorities, whether bishops, presbyteries, or synods? And was there a need to fill the office of bishop (overseer, superintendent) for the proper direction of the churches, thus establishing separate roles of bishop and presbyter? This concept was rejected by the congregational churches,[127] but later became a burning question in Wesleyan Methodism.

---

[124] "The Cambridge Platform 1648," in *The Reformation of the Church: A Collection of Reformed and Puritan Documents on Church Issues*, Iain Murray, ed. (London: Banner of Truth Trust, 1965), 247.

[125] This issue is discussed by Bradshaw in Wainwright, et. al in *Ordination Rites Past and Present.*

[126] Murray., 254.

[127] American Congregational churches did recognize the value of communion between established local churches and the synod's role of admonition in Article VX of the Cambridge Platform.

Wesley, of course, believed that "the world was his parish."[128]
And his ministry was extraordinary, indeed, in its trans-local
nature. But at the end of his life he had need to appoint overseers
for the far-flung movement his labors had spawned. So this
was one of the great questions for Wesley at the end of his life
and ministry. Were there three ministerial orders, as in classic
Catholicism and Anglicanism, or two? If two, then the need for a
bishop to exercise the ministry of ordaining presbyters was simply
a matter of custom. If there were three orders, then connection
with episcopal ordination was required for the legitimacy of the
emergent Methodist Church. This question had been addressed in
the fourth century by Jerome.

> This then we say to show that of old [*apud veteres*] the same
> persons were presbyters who were also bishops, but, little
> by little, that the seed-plots of dissension might be rooted
> up, all responsibility was conferred upon one. Therefore, as
> presbyters know that they are subject to him who is placed
> over them by the usage of the Church, so let the bishops know
> that they are greater than the presbyters rather by custom than
> by the verity of a divine appointment; and that they should
> rule the church in common, imitating Moses, who, when he
> had the power to rule alone over the people of Israel, chose
> the seventy, with whom to judge the people.[129]

Wesley, of course, chose to recognize only the orders of
deacon and presbyter. After Jerome's example, the role of overseer
and attendant authority to ordain was considered a function of
oversight rather than a separate episcopal order.

Accordingly, in 1784, a year after the formal recognition by
Great Britain of the independence of the United States, John

---

[128] John Wesley, *The Journal of John Wesley,* Percy Livingston Parker, ed.,
Chicago: Moody Press, n.d., 74.
[129] Jerome, Migne's *Patrologia Latina, xxvi,* 562 f., quoted in Thompson, 141.

Wesley and Thomas Coke, the latter also a priest (presbyter)
of the church of England, ordained two as presbyters ('elders')
for the United States and, assisted by other ministers, Wesley
set apart Coke as 'superintendent' for America and appointed
Francis Asbury, already in the United States, to a similar
office.[130]

Modern Catholicism sees the role of the ordained priesthood
as filling pastoral functions as well as the need for offering
sacrifice and forgiving sins. They are joined with, but subordinate
to, the episcopal order in fulfilling the ministry of Christ.[131] Thus
this distinction of order is maintained in the Catholic system.

Third Element: How Has the Church Traditionally Recognized Qualifications for Ministry Candidates?

What factors over the centuries have marked the church's
method of endorsing or eliminating candidates for ordained
ministry? Given the breadth of the survey, all relevant practices
cannot be fully addressed. It is self-evident that the method of
recognizing a candidate for ordination and the health of the church
go hand in hand. John Chrysostom summarizes the concerns of
the patristic church about the abuse of the selection process for
ordination:

[B]ut we ... have defiled it with so many pollutions, by
entrusting it to commonplace men who readily accept what
is offered them, without having first acquired a knowledge
of their own souls, or considered the gravity of the office,
and when they have entered on the work, being blinded by
inexperience, overwhelm with innumerable evils the people

---

[130] Kenneth Scott Latourette, *A History of Christianity,* Vol. II, (New York: Harper and Row, 1953, rev. 1975), 1028.
[131] "The Priesthood in the Church's Mission," in *Vatican Council II, The Conciliar and Post Conciliar Documents,* 864-5.

who have been committed to their care . . . . For, tell me, whence do you think such great troubles are generated in the Churches? I, for my part, believe the only source of them to be the inconsiderate and random way in which prelates are chosen and appointed.[132]

Again, Chrysostom expresses his concerns,

[O]ne is eager to give the preference to a man who is on terms of intimacy with himself, another to the man who is related to him by birth, a third to the flatterer, but no one will look to the man who is really qualified, or make some test of his character.[133]

Over a millennium later John Calvin expresses a similar concern when he writes, "Some owe their promotion to kindred or affinity, others to the influence of their parents . . . . In short, the end for which the offices are conferred is that provision may be made not for churches, but for those who receive them."[134]

Historically, several questions have been especially important in identifying ministerial candidates: 1) the role of personal or internal calling; 2) the character and motives of the potential ordinand; and 3) the trial of gifts and process of examination.

1. The Candidate's Sense of Internal Call

Does the candidate have a sense of internal call? The question of *internal call* has been addressed in varied ways throughout the history of the church. The issue is most prominent in the post-Reformation church. The early church emphasized the *external call* as a means of confirming God's call. This concept is covered later under the role of the congregation in the ordination process.

---

[132] Chrysostom, III, 10, 50.
[133] Ibid., III, 15, p. 53.
[134] *Institutes* IV, v, 6, p. 581.

The first element of ordination, that it is of God, implies a sense of internal calling. As stated above, this aspect is confirmed more in terms of outward recognition than internal witness in the patristic church. In fact, too eager an approach to the honor of the role of minister was seen in a negative light. This view led to the custom of forcible ordination.

Gregory Nazianzen, Chrysostom, his friend Basil, Ambrose, and Augustine all were conscripted into the service of the church as presbyters or bishops. One wonders whether an expected feigned humility or a genuine fear of God and esteem for the responsibilities of the pastoral role motivated these men to strenuously resist ordination. Ambrose's experience is common to the ancient world:

> After some years Auxentius, the intended Arian bishop of Milan, died, A.D. 374, and it is said that during the discussion as to the appointment of his successor a child cried out in the assembly, 'Ambrose Bishop,' and, although he was but a catechumen and so canonically unqualified, the multitude immediately elected him by acclamation.
>
> St. Ambrose did all in his power, even, . . . resorting to some questionable expedients, to escape from the dignity laid upon him, but when his election was ratified by the Emperor Valentinian, he recognized his appointment as being the will of God, and insisted on being baptized by a Catholic priest. Eight days later, December 7, A.D. 374, he was consecrated Bishop.[135]

Like Cyprian and Ambrose before him, Augustine was made presbyter against his will in 391 A.D. by the voice of the people. He was made bishop of Hippo Regius in North Africa in 395.[136]

---

[135] "Prolegomena to St. Ambrose," NPNF, Second Series, Vol. 10, p.xv.
[136] Philip Schaff, "Prolegomena: St. Augustin's Life and Work," Philip Schaff, ed. in NPNF, First Series, Vol. 1, 4-5.

The later church seems to have dispensed with the expected resistance to ordination. In fact, for Calvin the sense of internal calling is a mark of legitimacy. In describing the secret call, he says, "I mean the good testimony of our heart, that we undertake the office neither from ambition nor avarice, nor any other selfish feeling, but a sincere fear of God, and desire to edify the Church."[137] Similar to the ancient method, though, the Cambridge Platform sees the summons of the church as the confirmation of one's call to ministry, as opposed to an immediate or personal call.[138]

Thomas Oden, in his *Pastoral Theology,* states a more contemporary approach this way: "Do not act too quickly on such a momentous first impression. Let an initial impression grow quietly in a community of prayer until it becomes a sustained conviction."[139]

This leads to the question: What of those who express a sense of calling, but have no confirmation or endorsement from others? Generally, all traditions require an external call or endorsement of both the community and existing spiritual leaders. Oden writes, "If the answer has to be no, it should not be defensively received or harshly given."[140] This "no" often has been based on examination of the candidate in terms of character, motive, gifts, and theological knowledge.

---

[137] *Institutes,* IV, iii, 11, p. 567.

[138] Cambridge Platform, VIII, 1-2, *The Reformation of the Church*, 252.

[139] Oden, 18. Oden also advises the careful investigation of special providence in one's sense of call. "Can or should alleged special inspiration be examined? How far is it possible or desirable for an ecclesiastical examining body to seek to assess alleged providential events or personal revelations that may have influenced a candidate's conception of ministry or calling? Such special 'leadings' need to be sensitively explored with reserved good judgment." (p. 24).

[140] Ibid., 20. "Those who hear an outward no to their inwardly felt call should not forget how difficult these decisions are for others to make."

2. Character and Motives of the Ordinand

Much has been made throughout church history of both
the character and motives of those seeking ordination in the
church. Concepts of suitability are based on Biblical criteria as
well as developed traditions. In the Apostolic Constitutions, the
patristic church looked carefully into both aspects of a candidate's
qualifications.

> But concerning bishops, we have heard from our Lord, that
> a pastor who is to be ordained a bishop for the churches in
> every parish, must be unblameable, unreprovable, free from
> all kinds of wickedness common among men, not under fifty
> years of age; for such a one is in good part past youthful
> disorders . . . .[141]

Often the Canons are informed by Biblical criteria such as
those found in I Timothy and Titus. "Let him therefore be sober,
prudent, decent, firm, stable, not given to wine; no striker, but
gentle; not a brawler, not covetous . . . ."[142]

Chrysostom and Gregory the Great both recognize the power
of character as help or hindrance to ministry, particularly any hint
of the lust for power.

> [H]is soul ought to be thoroughly purged from any lust after
> the office; for if he happens to have a natural inclination for
> this dignity, as soon as he attains it a stronger flame is kindled
> and the man being taken completely captive will endure
> innumerable evils in order to keep a secure hold on it, even
> to the extent of using flattery, or submitting to something
> base and ignoble, or expending large sums of money.[143]

---

[141] Apostolic Constitutions, II, i,396.

[142] Ibid. II, I,396.

[143] Chrysostom, III, 10,50. Chrysostom also addresses the damage of a poor
example in the place of leadership. "For the mass of people under government

And, again, Chrysostom states, "Now I have not said that it is
a terrible thing to desire the *work*, but only the authority and
power."[144]

Gregory the Great, in the patristic tradition, recognized the
danger of twisting scripture to hide selfish motives in pursuing
the ministry of the Church. "But for the most part those who
covet pre-eminence seize on the language of the Apostle where
he says, 'If a man desire the office of a bishop, he desireth a good
work.'"[145]

The question of character, tested in the crucible of close
relationships, was important from the earliest times. Thus the
Apostolic Constitutions:

> In this manner let examination be made when he is to receive
> ordination, and to be placed in his bishopric, whether he
> be grave, faithful, decent; whether he have a grave and
> faithful wife, or has formerly had such a one; whether he
> hath educated his children piously, and has 'brought them
> up in the nurture and admonition of the Lord'; whether his
> domestics do fear and reverence him, and are all obedient to
> him: for if those who are immediately about him for worldly
> concerns are seditious and disobedient, how will others not

---

are generally inclined to regard the manners of those who govern as a kind of
model type, and to assimilate themselves to them....but the errors of a man in
a conspicuous position, and known to many, inflicts a common injury upon
all, rendering those who have fallen more supine in their efforts for good, and
driving to desperation those who wish to take heed to themselves" (III, 14, 52).
Chrysostom also speaks to the issue of youthfulness as a negative consideration
but not an absolute prohibition, "[T]hat the young man ought not to be
absolutely excluded from the ministry, but only the novice: and the difference
between the two is great" (II, 8, 44).

[144] Ibid. III, 11, 50.

[145] Gregory the Great, "The Book of Pastoral Rule," I, viii, in NPNF, Second
Series, Vol. 12, 5. Book I of Gregory's classic covers all of the questions of
suitable gifts, calling, motive, reasons for fleeing ordination, and clarifications
of when this is noble and when ignoble.

of his family, when they are under his management, become obedient to him?[146]

Of particular interest here is the behavior of those closest to the candidate.

The area of character presumably includes a kind of aptitude or suitability for working with people. As Oden states, "The candidates should have personal gifts for ministry. These include a realistic self-awareness, the ability to work patiently with others, love, compassion, and respect for other people."[147] In addition he says, "The candidate's good character should be affirmed by those who know the candidate best." [148]

3. The Trial of Gifts and Process of Examination

There is a clear overlap in the literature of the church between examination of character and examination of giftedness and knowledge for ministry. Character is being tried while giftedness is on trial. Theological knowledge and sound doctrine are integral to the process as well. The Apostolic Constitutions address both issues of character and education.

> Let him therefore, if it be possible, be well educated; but if he be unlettered, let him at any rate be skillful in the word, and of competent age. But if in a small parish one advanced in years is not to be found, let some younger person, who has a good report among his neighbors, and is esteemed by them worthy of the office of a bishop, who has carried himself from his youth with meekness and regularity, like a much elder person, after examination, and a general good report, be ordained in peace.[149]

---

[146] Apostolic Constitutions II, ii, 396-7
[147] Oden, 22.
[148] Ibid.
[149] Apostolic Constitutions, II, i, ANF, Vol. 7, 396.

An examination of a candidate's theological knowledge and education becomes a pillar of Reformed practice. The lack of an examination of biblical and doctrinal knowledge in Calvin's time draws severe criticism in the *Institutes.*

> Any examination of doctrine is too old fashioned, but if any respect is had to doctrine, they make choice of some lawyer who knows better how to plead in the forum than to preach in the church. This much is certain, that for a hundred years, scarcely one in a hundred has been elected who had any acquaintance with sacred doctrine.[150]

Calvin here addresses the complaint of the Reformation church of a neglect of doctrinal knowledge within the priesthood generally.

Fourth Element: What is the Role of Spiritual Authorities in the Process of Ordination?

It is clear that throughout church history, existing spiritual authorities played a primary role – actually, *the* primary role – in recognizing new ministers. Beginning with the concept of apostolic succession in the patristic church, the participation of existing bishops, priests, or ministers has been a *sine qua non* (requirement) for ordination in all except the most non-traditional (not to say *anti*-traditional) of free churches.

Even in the church of the first three centuries, where congregational participation in candidate selection was expected, the role of existing leaders was the primary mover throughout the process. Later, during medieval times, congregational involvement diminished due to the increased clerical role in choosing candidates.[151] Even after the restoration of congregational

---

[150] *Institutes*, IV, v, 1, 579

[151] *Institutes*, IV, v, 2., 579. "Then, in election, the whole right has been taken from the people. Vows, assents, subscriptions, and all things of this sort, have disappeared; the whole power has been given to the canons alone. First, they

participation in the Reformation period, the existing ministry played a primary role both in candidate selection and examination and in the rite of ordination itself.[152]

Of course, the question of adequate spiritual authority in the naming of ministry successors was first addressed by Clement of Rome at Corinth. By establishing apostolic succession, the question of legitimacy was tied to recognition by existing leadership. The bishops lists kept by Hegesippus, Irenaeus, and Eusebius likewise tied legitimacy to recognition. In essence, ordination, at its very core, consists of the blessing of existing spiritual leadership.[153]

It was in the Donatist controversy that the adequacy of spiritual authorities themselves first came to the fore regarding ordination. The church in North Africa addressed the issue of the purity of those who administer ordination (along with other sacraments in the Latin Catholic tradition). The *traditore* bishops who had failed in the persecution were considered unworthy spiritual authorities.[154] Their participation in the rite of blessing contaminated the ordination of Caecilian in the early fourth century. This led to over a century of wrangling about questions of legitimacy. For our purpose it is important to recognize the source of the controversy. To wit, proper spiritual authority is required for legitimate ordination. Augustine's doctrine *ex opere operato,* mentioned in the introduction, resolved the dispute. Nevertheless, appropriate spiritual authority has always been an issue in ordination.

---

confer the episcopal office on whomever they please; by-and-by they bring him forth into the view of the people, but it is to be adored, not examined."
[152] *Institutes,* IV, iii, 15, p. 569. "Other pastors, however, ought to preside over the election, lest any error should be committed by the general body either through levity, or bad passion, or tumult."
[153] See discussion of the term *samakh* in the literature review, particularly Everett Ferguson in "The Laying on of Hands: Its Significance in Ordination" (1975).
[154] *Traditores* were bishops who had apostasized during the Diocletian persecution by handing over copies of sacred Scriptures to be destroyed.

The Canons and the Apostolic Constitutions clearly establish who may participate in the ordination rite itself, requiring the presence of at least two neighboring bishops for episcopal ordination. [155] Chrysostom, in common with other patristic writers, warns against misuse of one's leadership position, especially in relation to the ordination process. "He who is going to ordain, therefore, ought to make diligent inquiry . . . . For he who gives authority to anyone who is minded to destroy the Church, would be certainly to blame for the outrages which that person commits."[156]

Calvin goes into some detail on the issue, both endorsing the need for ministerial participation in ordination and endorsing congregational participation. Commenting on the Council of Laodicea, he writes:

> For, first, the clergy alone selected, and presented him whom they had selected to the magistrate, or senate, and chief men. These, after deliberation, put their signature to the election, if it seemed proper, if not, they chose another whom they more highly approved. The matter was then laid before the multitude, who, although not bound by those previous proceedings, were less able to act tumultuously.[157]

In fact, the central role of existing spiritual leadership in recognizing, nurturing, testing, approving, and ordaining new pastors is the single most widely recognized practice associated with ordination.

This begs the question: What of those who are not so recognized? While many systems require the approval of existing ministries as *the* primary means of legitimacy, most reform movements, of necessity, arise in the context of non-recognition, or even condemnation. This consideration is precisely what

---

[155] Canon iv of Nicaea requires the presence of three and the suffrage of all bishops of a province.

[156] Chrysostom, IV, 2, 63.

[157] *Institutes,* IV, iv, 12, 575-6.

moved Quakers, Puritans (both Presbyterian and Independent), Anabaptists, and various free churches to reject apostolic succession as well as the authority of then-existing clergy regarding ordination in many cases. This is especially so when the existing system and its *ministerium* are seen as corrupt. Nevertheless, even the new emerging reform movements tend to establish a system of recognition through existing spiritual leaders.[158]

Fifth Element: Is There a Rite Associated with Ordination through Church History?

Like biblical ordination, a rite is associated with the recognition of spiritual leadership throughout church history. The rite takes different forms and may include diverse features, yet many elements are fairly constant. This treatment divides aspects of the rite into prayer, laying on of hands (or a substitute), various symbols, sermon or charge, and recognition of or impartation of grace.

The oldest ordination prayer is the prayer of Hippolytus quoted earlier in the chapter under segment one, "Is the Ordination of God?" In fact, prayer for the ordinand is a constant of the ordination rite, whether uttered by the bishop, ordaining ministers, or the congregation. It may take the form of a hymn petitioning for God's grace such as "Come, Holy Ghost."[159]

In many ordination services several prayers were used. Two invocations which have been both common and controversial are "Receive the Holy Ghost" and "Whosoever's sins ye remit shall be remitted," both based on Christ's post-resurrection encounter with his disciples in John's Gospel (20:22-3). These prayers have

---

[158] Even in the case of the early church, witness the emergence of a more defined church polity after the *Didache* at the time of the Apostolic Fathers.

[159] J.H. Crehan, "Medieval Ordinations" in *The Study of Liturgy*, contains a complete table of ordination practices used in Western Europe by the 10th century.

been used to confirm the priestly nature of ordination and were resisted by the Puritans as remnants of the Roman system.[160]

Laying on of hands has been the primary act associated with ordination. In the time of the Reformation it was abandoned in some cases, again because of its association with Roman Catholicism and the implications of mechanical impartation of the Spirit. So, in some cases, giving of the right hand of fellowship was used in its place.[161]

Other practices directly related to ordination were the seating (as mentioned in Chapter Two) of the candidate after the blessing. This was used especially in the case of bishops who took their *cathedra* in order to govern the church, though it may have been used in non-episcopal ordination as well. Laying on of hands was also accompanied by anointing with oil in some cases.[162]

Additional symbols were used in various locales and eras, but established no single pattern. Some of these symbols included laying the Gospels on the neck or holding them over the head of the candidate; giving the Gospels or the Bible to the candidate; clothing him in special robes; giving a ring, a staff, a paten, or a chalice; exchanging the kiss of peace; and in the case of bishops, conferring a miter.[163]

Of course, Reformation rites discarded some of these practices, but often included a sermon or charge to the ordinand and congregation based on Scripture. Prayer and fasting was enjoined by the Savoy Platform.

One of the more controversial questions concerned whether ordination imparted special grace to the recipient. That it did was

---

[160] See Paul F. Bradshaw, "The Reformers and the Ordination Rites," in *Ordination rites Past and Present,* 105, for a discussion.
[161] Ibid.104.
[162] J.H. Crehan, "Medieval Ordinations" in *The Study of Liturgy*, contains a complete table of ordination practices used in Western Europe by the 10th century.
[163] Crehan, McEachern, Bradshaw, and Frank Hawkins (in *The Study of Liturgy)* among others detail various forms used in ordination rites.

taken for granted in the Catholic system. Grace was conferred through apostolic succession. The authority to forgive sins and the ability to celebrate the Eucharist eventually became the impartation of an indelible character.[164]

The Protestant system under Calvin's leadership rejected the idea of impartation as too mystical and removed any sacramental powers from ordination, or Holy Orders as it is called in Catholicism.[165] Baptist views of ordination take a similar tack, viewing ordination as recognition of grace gifts already given rather than impartation.

Also, the rite may be viewed as a reflection of polity. Episcopal ordination systems require episcopal participation; Presbyterian, participation of elders; and Congregational, technically, participation of only the congregation. In practice, the existing ministry administrates or presides in Congregational ordination.

Sixth Element: How is the Congregation Involved in the Rite and Result of Ordination?

Congregational participation in the process of ordination has been variously understood throughout church history. In the patristic church, a process of recognition and consultation that included the congregation was prominent, both in the choice of the candidate and in the ordination rite itself. As noted earlier, candidates were often ordained by popular acclaim and sometimes against their will. As Cyprian stated, it was the custom of bishops to consult with the people concerning the choice of those who would minister to them. A mark of the Reformation churches was their insistence on congregational input in identifying recipients of the pastoral office.

---

[164] McEachern, 37.

[165] Calvin addresses the issue of Orders as a sacrament in detail in *Institutes* IV, xix, 22-33.

Congregational involvement covers three basic areas: 1) the selection of the candidate; 2) participation in the rite; and 3) change in relationship.

1. Selection of the candidate

As noted previously, congregational input was sought in the patristic and Reformation churches. Calvin traces the developments in this area as follows:

> "Those examples," says Cyprian, "show that the ordination of a priest behooved not to take place, unless under the consciousness of the people assisting, so that ordination was just and legitimate which was vouched by the testimony of all." We see, then, that ministers are legitimately called according to the word of God, when those who may have seemed fit are elected on the consent and approbation of the people. Other pastors, however, ought to preside over the election, lest any error should be committed by the general body either through levity, or bad passion, or tumult.[166]

Calvin repeatedly insists on the necessity of popular suffrage as a part of the process of ordination, and decries its evolution into an appointment process bypassing the voice of the congregation. (See *Institutes,* IV, iv, 14-15). For this reason, Reformation ordinations were always done in public, generally on Sundays, in the midst of the congregation that was to receive the ministry of the ordained person. This arrangement was in contrast to medieval ordinations, which had become private matters needing only the participation of the bishop,[167] thus removing the people from the process altogether, as Calvin complained.

---

[166] *Institutes,* IV, iii, 15, p. 569.
[167] Bradshaw, 104.

Calvin also spoke of the process of gaining public approval, which he endorsed as a superior method of choosing ministers:

> (F)or no sub-deacon was appointed who had not given a long proof of his conduct in the clerical office, agreeable to the strictness of discipline then in use. After he had approved himself in that degree, he was appointed deacon, and thereafter, if he conducted himself faithfully, he attained to the honor of a presbyter. Thus none were promoted whose conduct had not, in truth, been tested for many years under the eye of the people....In fine, all ordinations took place at stated periods of the year, that none might creep in stealthily *without the consent of the faithful,* or be promoted with too much facility without witnesses" (emphasis mine).[168]

This element was crucial in the development of Calvin's doctrine of ordination and in documents such as the Savoy Platform (1658), one of the most congregational of the Reformed documents. "The way appointed by Christ for the calling of any person, fitted and gifted by the Holy Ghost, unto the office of pastor, teacher, or elder in a church, is, that he be chosen thereunto by the common suffrage of the church itself . . ."[169]

This congregational participation is a primary feature of free churches with congregational polity. The concept of suffrage has strong affirmation in numerous Reformed documents as well as early church practice (Cyprian quoted in Calvin, for example). Oden, from a Methodist perspective, recognizes community participation at an early stage through the activity of ordination

---

[168] *Institutes,* IV, iv, 10, 575.
[169] "The Savoy Platform" in *The Reformation of the Church*, p. 277. Note the reference to 'fitting and gifting of the Holy Ghost,' acknowledging that the ordination is *of God.*

committees that have the power to encourage or discourage (even veto) a candidate for ministry.[170]

2. Participation in the Rite

As noted by Bradshaw above, the Reformation pattern of ordination was a public rite in the presence of the congregation. It usually included a public charge and/or sermon recounting the duties of ordained ministry. The public nature of the service was characteristic of the patristic era as well. The congregation was present for the prayers and confirmed the candidate through the affirmation "He is worthy."[171]

As noted above, the private ordination accompanied the removal of the congregation's input during the medieval period. Congregational participation was vigorously defended by the reformers. In contemporary Baptist ordinations, the entire congregation may be invited to lay hands on the minister as a mark of their participation in the process from beginning to end.[172]

3. Change in relationship

Historically, the ordinand's relationship with the congregation changes when he gains the authority to govern and the power to preside in the ministry of word and sacrament (in most systems). Authority to govern includes the remission and retaining of sins (in the Catholic system) as well as directing the process of censure and correction. Richard Baxter dealt with this issue in some detail in *The Reformed Pastor.*

In essence, the ordination entails, at least implicitly, a recognition by the congregation of the minister's authority to lead both governmentally and liturgically. This includes, as stated in the

---

[170] Oden, 20.

[171] This carried over through medieval times, McEachern, 36.

[172] Ibid.,47.

section on the role of spiritual authorities, the prerogative to take the lead in recognizing and establishing new ministers.

This charge or power gives the ordained pastor a position of leadership within the congregation that is recognized by existing leadership and the people as one of primary importance in the life of the congregation.

A good statement of the wider church's view of the ordination process is found in a contemporary publication, the *Confession of Faith in a Mennonite Perspective*:

> The act of ordination symbolizes a combination of God's call, the congregation's affirmation, the recipient's dedication to ministry, and the blessing of the wider church. Ordination follows a process of discernment in the congregation and in the wider church or conference. [173]

This statement captures much of the sentiment and practice of the Christian church expressed through various confessions and historical circumstances.

---

[173] *Confession of Faith in a Mennonite Perspective,* (Scottsdale, PA: Herald Press, 1995), 61.

Chapter Six
Recommended Practices for
Evangelical Churches

Given the information from the previous two chapters, what can we say about the practice of ordination for churches today? Traditional churches have their practices in place. They most likely include the six essential elements in their process of developing and confirming candidates for spiritual leadership. Nevertheless, both traditional and non-denominational churches could benefit from comparing their practices with these essentials.

Contemporary non-denominational churches have a special challenge in this area. They have no tradition to draw from but claim to base their practices on scripture. Yet many non-denominational churches have given little thought to questions concerning ordination. An intentional process would provide great benefit. In addition to the need for legitimation, which ultimately comes from the Spirit of God, there is a need to conform to biblical practice, if not historical tradition.

Should anyone who happens to claim an "anointing" be received as a legitimate minister of Christ? Is testing of character and doctrine to be dispensed with because individuals make spiritual claims for themselves? Is the flock at the mercy of the self-anointed, or should a biblical guideline be in place to protect the flock of Christ and guide the process, both preventing fraud and confirming giftedness? Common sense and the Bible both say a guiding process is in order.

On the other hand, legitimacy is not a question of human

approval, especially in the case of truly prophetic ministry. By *prophetic* I mean the call to announce tidings which may challenge and bring discomfort to the status quo, or confront corruption in existing church systems. In such cases, the normally healthy vetting processes described in the chapters above may thwart a needed call to repentance and change.

When putting forward practical applications for the contemporary church, it is important to remember that some of the six elements are missing in many biblical and historical examples. Consequently, I am not seeking to establish a new canon or list of rules on ordination, but rather to provide guidelines for those who could benefit from them. Based on the foregoing study of the Bible and history, here are some concluding thoughts and recommendations.

First Element: Reliance upon God

A question every church leadership team or eldership needs to ask itself is: Is the Spirit of God the initiating force for the ordination process? Is there a genuine sense that God is involved in the process of recognition, development, and confirmation of those filling ministry roles? Is the church community recognizing a God-given gifting and call, or just conforming to an established system, or filling a need out of expediency?

Apart from God's blessing, the ordination or recognition process is in vain. That is not to say that it is harmless. Shepherds give or take, feed or devour. Failure to recognize the Holy Spirit's role in calling and establishing ministry (ordained or not) exposes the church to significant danger. Ensuring this understanding is essential to the art of encouraging and ordaining new leadership.

Therefore, a local church community or ministry must see itself as having been called into existence by the Lord Himself. It must see that yielding to gifted leaders is essential to its welfare. And it must recognize that the role of ministry is one filled with both positive and negative potential. To yield one's heart to the ministrations of another is required in church life, yet the yielding is also conditional. "And you should follow my example, just *as I follow Christ's*" (I Cor. 10:1 TLB, emphasis mine) is the counsel of the apostle. Another warning against unconditional acceptance: "But even if we or an angel from heaven should preach a gospel other than the one we preached to you, let him be accursed" (Gal.1:8 ESV). It is foolish to think that the choice of a pastor, elder, or other influential servant of the church and the message they preach is an inconsequential decision. So, the witness of the Spirit, however recognized, is essential to true, healthy ordination.

This process requires a commitment to serious and ongoing prayer on the part of the church or ministry. The level of prayerfulness and spiritual hunger will most likely determine a church's ability to discern and receive the kind of minister in keeping with congregational need.

This determination entails more than just the *who* but the *when* and the *how* as well. Issues such as who is encouraged to serve in teaching and pastoral ministry, the timing of their endorsement, and the opportunity for wide recognition are at issue here. Even leaders of neighboring churches must be given opportunity to affirm a pastor's giftedness – that is, if they are expected to participate in an ordination rite, laying on hands of blessing and endorsement. At the least this cooperation implies participation in a vicinage (from vicinity or region) council or regional ordination committee with a meaningful examination process.

Prayer by the individual, the existing leadership, and the wider church, testing of personal calling and gifts, the affirmation of spiritual authorities and confirmation by the wider community, including leaders of other churches, all offer a means of confirming this first great question: Is the ordination of God?

So what are the hindrances to the recognition of the divine role in the process? One of the first hindrances, historically at least, has been ecclesiastical fiat. Existing leaders without concern for prayer or a process of spiritual discernment use their role in the process to usurp the place of God's call, replacing it with a mechanical, humanistic system.

A similar but opposite hindrance to a God-ordained process is congregational fiat. The popularity of an individual is sufficient to carry an election based not on a process of discernment, but on simple popular suffrage. In the worst-case scenario, a carnal political process accompanies the appointment. The lay investiture controversies of the Middle Ages were examples of powerful or wealthy lay leaders controlling the ministerial appointment process to conform with their own, often worldly, wishes to the exclusion of God-chosen candidates.

Another hindrance is yielding to one who practices self-appointment. Ministry is received, not seized. A call to serve a congregation is an invitation extended, not a right demanded. The process involves a gift and call recognized, not a self-fulfilled prophecy. In essence, "Truly, truly, I say to you, he who does not enter the sheepfold by the door, but climbs in by another way, that man is a thief and robber. But he who enters by the door is the shepherd of the sheep" (John 10:1-2 ESV). The true shepherd trustingly passes through the gate opened by the Spirit of God and is affirmed by the process of the essential elements of ordination (or a preponderance of them). The self-appointed enters through the window of self-affirmation rather than the Spirit's witness.

It is my experience in the charismatic movement that this is one of the most widespread abuses of the ministerial appointment process. The reason seems to be that charismatics fear quenching the Spirit. They are timid about calling a self-announced prophet into question. But in fact, they are called to "Test everything. Hold on to the good" (I Thess. 5:21 NIV). Instead, they grieve the Spirit by failing to adequately protect Christ's flock from predators.

It is prayerfulness that can ensure that the Holy Spirit's leadership is honored. A praying leadership and church body give place to the leadership of Christ the head. Prayer in the selection and confirmation process of the church's ministry recognizes God's role in choosing His servants. Prayerful deliberation prior to recognition and blessing of pastoral ministers is the most crucial element in following a God-given pattern for ordination.

A Need for a Specific Ministry

A church needs to ask itself: What purpose does ordination serve? What role does it play in the community? If the church blesses its ministers for the sake of the community, then it's on the right track. The ordination process should be driven (after assurance of God's favor) by the need of the community for a specific kind of recognized leadership. But often, in a distortion of the event, it is driven by the need of the candidate to be recognized, validated, or – most crassly – afforded tax-exempt status.

If all are a priesthood of believers, then there must be a specific reason to set apart an elder or pastor that relates to the need of the congregation. The purpose is not to recognize a person's giftedness or to affirm simply for the sake of affirmation. Rather, a Spirit-initiated process is intended to establish a biblical pattern of ministry to the congregation.

This brings into question the concept of the at-large ordination. While it would be appropriate for communities to recognize previous ordinations, it is also important to recognize that ministry is valid in the context of a community, even if that community is the wider un-evangelized society.

Some expect to carry their credentials with them from congregation to congregation, so that an elder or pastor ordained in one city expects recognition or admission to leadership upon joining another congregation hundreds of miles away. The person's giftedness may be the same, but congregational need has changed, not to mention questions of trust and recognition. Fresh recognition by the new body and affirmation by its leadership is needed for valid ministry.

At-large ordination is valid to the extent that there is a need in the wider community for the trans-local teacher, evangelist, prophet, or apostle. This does not mean that ministry of the word may take place only under the auspices of the ordination. On the contrary, ministry is validated by giftedness, not ordination. This custom of limiting ordination to filling a recognized need places no restriction on ministry, only on claims of entitlement to leadership positions.

The problem is that ordination can be a candidate-driven process. Candidate needs may range from desire for personal recognition to a need for a job. Such considerations short-circuit the broader essentials. This is true for self-invited pulpiteers, as well. Most pastors have encountered any number of seminary-trained or previously ordained persons who believe their education or past experience entitles them to a regular turn in the pulpit when they take up residence n a new place. Such thinking betrays a fundamental misunderstanding of the nature of ministry.

True ministry is welcomed by the community. There is a reciprocal affirmation. This, of course, does not invalidate prophetic ministry, which may never be embraced by the affected community or its leaders. Nevertheless, simply put, ministry is not a right demanded by candidates, nor a privilege bestowed by ecclesiastical authorities, but a mix, even a mystery, of the essential elements of Spirit-bestowed giftedness and wide agreement of the community coming together to edify a needy people to the glory of God.

Here many make a mistake. Ordination is appropriate only because there is a specific need in the congregation recognized by the leadership. The ordination process is never to be held captive to the expedient desires of potential candidates, or even the impatient insistence of the community. Ordination is a blessing bestowed, not a right claimed. This goes with invitations to serve in a pulpit through the ministry of the Word as well.

This does not mean that legitimate requests to be recognized should be suppressed. To desire the work, as the apostle says, is a noble thing. But there is a delicate balance between the boldness of desire and the insolence of selfish ambition. This is the discernment responsibility of the existing ministry leaders and congregation.

Effective, fruitful, gifted, God-empowered ministry is
perfectly possible *without* the benefit of ordination and it may be
welcomed by existing leaders. At the same time, all the apostolic
ordinations in the world cannot confer God's favor. From a truly
biblical free church perspective, withholding ordination does not
eliminate a believer's position as a priest, nor does it prevent God
from bestowing gifts as He chooses. Ordination does empower
the effectiveness of a ministry through congregational acceptance
and agreement, however. Premature recognition will not foster this
benefit, but may actually hinder it, as in, say, I Timothy 3:6, where
premature ordination leads to overweening pride.

Recognition of Candidates

The process of ordination is a matter of identifying God-
gifted servants of the body of Christ. That is not to say that
ordination is a requirement for ministry. It is not. But the local
church or wider ministry needs recognized and gifted ministers of
the Word. So the process of ordination involves identification.

Identification is normally achieved through ongoing
relationship. Such relationships with mentors and congregants
create opportunity to prove gifts, demonstrate strength of character
(or flaws), grow in knowledge and experience, and win the trust,
respect, and confidence of the believing community.

An ongoing relationship affords opportunity for spiritual
growth as well as hands-on service opportunities; it also offers
guidance in academic and doctrinal training. In this way a
candidate's personal sense of call and character can be tested in a
congregational setting. Several areas should be scrutinized over a
period of years. Much of this kind of scrutiny has been delegated
to seminaries in the traditional model, but ongoing congregational
life continues to be the best crucible for congregational skills. The
component of doctrinal skill is probably better added in a more
formal setting, though.

Numerous character questions should be addressed in

the development of spiritual leaders. Some things to watch for: extreme insecurity (ministry is *the* source of one's self-worth), manipulation, bristling under correction, not accepting disappointment well, presumption, arrogance, false doctrine, verbal dishonesty (lying), financial dishonesty (cheating), life-controlling habits such as nicotine, alcohol, or pornography, forward or injudicious behavior toward the opposite or same sex, abusive behavior toward spouse or subordinates, plagiarism, creating cliques, use of prophecy to control or manipulate, and a track record of failed relationships or failed ministry. And, as one pastor put it, "If you're too big to follow, you're too little to lead."

When do these troubling traits disqualify? They disqualify when they do not respond to correction and clearly hinder a candidate's ability to lead a ministry. This is a matter of discernment for spiritual leaders. These things may not always be readily evident to all. For this reason the congregation confirms the process rather than guiding it. In fact, there are numerous stories where the dishonest or unethical minister maintains the most devoted following despite misconduct and warnings or discipline from existing leaders.

On a positive note, these traits should be present: love for God and His people, a desire for the work, proven ability in leadership and administrative skills, scrupulous honesty, high ethical standards, aptitude in teaching or preaching, an ability to relate positively to people, especially co-workers and those in the household, sensitivity to spiritual matters, prayerfulness, knowledge of God's Word, ability to gain and keep the respect of congregants of varied experience, social strata, or vocation, and long-term success in relationships or ministry assignments. This is to name only a few traits of import.

How long should leaders be trained? Training should be of sufficient duration for spiritual leaders to know the person relationally and to surface, address, and work through issues already cited. Training should be long enough to test gifts and build the confidence of existing leaders and a receptive community.

And training should be long enough for God to demonstrate his favor in the person's life. The questions cannot be answered mechanically. On the other hand, the probationary period should not be too long. Do not pass up the opportunity to affirm and establish the new pastor within the community that needs pastoral ministry.

Seminary training has been the traditional model for ministerial preparation. But formal training apart from a believing community, and by that I mean a local church, impoverishes the process of nurture prescribed in scripture. Fresh models of cooperation between the local or regional church and the rigors of academic discipline offered by seminaries are needed to continue both the biblical pattern and historic tradition.

Participation of Spiritual Authorities

The spiritual leaders of a church or ministry carry primary responsibility for the health, growth, and development of the believing community. The rite of ordination is essentially a matter of placing their blessing on a new generation of stewards of Christ's church. Scripture is clear that there is a personal responsibility in the process, especially if sinful behavior is enabled thereby. If existing eldership is responsible to oversee the process of identification, development, and ordination of new leaders, then intentionality is appropriate.

Pastors and elders should be mindful of those under their care who exhibit aptitude for greater responsibility in the body of Christ. They should provide a context where ministry can emerge, mentoring can take place, giftedness can be tried and affirmed in smaller, and then larger settings. It is of first importance that leaders take counsel together and recognize the witness of the Spirit confirming the character and giftedness of a candidate, and address potential problem areas. Periods of prayer and fasting for guidance in this matter have both biblical and historical precedent.

Potential pastors need to see in their elders those who would encourage and mentor them. Elders should be open to an approach from one called to a teaching, pastoral, or other ministry in the church. They should take the lead in encouraging those who express a sense of calling and help them ask hard questions of themselves. If satisfied that a candidate needs to be encouraged, they should take the lead in forming a mentoring team. The team should be composed of mature Christians who have handled responsibilities in the church, who have experience and wisdom in life, in church, and with people. They should be capable of honest interaction and have the candidate's best interest at heart. In this way they should be involved in guiding the process of spiritual nurture of future leaders.

There are some hindrances to effectual leadership in the matter of mentoring the next generation. These have to do with methods and motives. If church history is any guide, congregations need to be partners in affirming emerging leaders. Unwillingness by spiritual leaders to recognize the competence of the people of God (the priesthood of all believers) in this matter hinders an effective process. In the same vein, leaders who refuse to take counsel of other leaders and open the process to a wider presbytery may be inviting problems, simply for lack of counsel and expanded insight.

Ordination is blessing by the existing leadership. This blessing must be given sincerely, not prematurely, and without regret. Some may err on the side of laxity. Other leaders may exercise inordinate control of the process. Resisting the clear sense of God's favor may result from too restrictive a view of the place of ordination. Some may be protecting selfish interests. Self-examination is necessary. On the other hand, apart from regional and congregational input, inappropriate favoritism may be shown. Mentors may be blind to the flaws of a favored co-worker or disciple.

Premature ordination, or ordination of the unqualified, is not irreversible, but the need for removal of credentials is a process best avoided at the outset. Refusing ordination is better than a possibly contentious process of confrontation and censure. Such procedures, and the events which precipitate them, tend to demoralize the church. Scripture warns against irresponsible promotion. "Like tying a stone in a sling is the giving of honor to a fool" (Prov. 26:8 NIV); and "Like an archer who wounds at random is he who hires a fool or any passer-by" (Prov. 26:10 NIV). Better to have candidates exercise their gifts successfully without formal recognition than to offer formal recognition to those who will abuse the privilege of leadership and bring disgrace to the church and ministry.

Pastors should take care to live up to the requirements of equipping a new generation of leaders. They should examine their leadership styles to see whether they encourage the identification and development of new leadership. They should make training in character and doctrine a priority. Regional training and ordination councils would contribute to this process immensely. Another option is a close collaboration between existing seminaries, local churches, and regional movements.

Rite

An ordination rite should be performed in the midst of the congregation which will receive the ministry of the ordained. The Reformation practice of ordaining during the regular Sunday morning service is suitable, but a Sunday evening service may be conducive to participation by the regional church. Many churches choose a candidate's previous church or a conference meeting. These are customary in many cases, but the setting of the receiving church seems most in keeping with the spirit and purpose of ordination.

Spiritual leaders of the existing congregation should certainly participate. Past leaders who have moved away but who may be available and in good standing would add a strong statement of honor and continuity with the congregation's past. Local pastors and leaders of the movement or denomination add the witness, participation, and blessing of the wider regional church. All of this adds to the meaning and effectiveness of the rite, especially in the eyes of the congregation.

The rite normally would take place in the context of a worship service planned specifically for the purpose of ordination. The rite should include worship, prayer, public reading and preaching from Scripture, and a charge, including questions concerning the call and commitment of the new pastor and congregation to the pastoral relationship. Laying on of hands should be carried out by the ministers present, with congregational participation where appropriate. A recognized spiritual leader clearly connected to the congregation should preside at the meeting.

The service must acknowledge belief that God is the author of true empowerment for ministry, and the Holy Spirit the one who bestows gifts. The rite of laying on of hands is a significant spiritual exercise. Expectation of additional empowerment by the Spirit with words of encouragement or prophetic impartation should accompany the outward sign of the laying on of hands.

Various ministries and congregations may wish to add elements to the service. These may include the giving of symbolic gifts from the congregation (in token of recognition and acceptance), testimonials from the candidate or mentor concerning one's sense of calling to this ministry, or an exhortation from the new pastor. At any rate the ordinand should address the congregation, at least briefly, in some form.

As in all the essential elements, the goal is not to keep to a specific script for the rite, but to give place to the leadership of God's Spirit and to establish God-ordained ministry. The best ways to establish a biblical ordination rite are to encourage broad public participation in the context of a worship service using time-honored symbols of ordination (laying on of hands, prayer, etc.), and to provide a place for public affirmation by spiritual leaders reflecting careful deliberation over the candidate and the congregation's need.

Congregation

The Reformers expected a congregation to recognize its shepherd. This belief was foundational to Reformation practice of ordination. Sheep recognize the voice of the shepherd. Nevertheless, just like spiritual leaders, a congregation may err. In the Bible and history, the process of choosing leaders is guided by existing leadership. But to eliminate congregational input creates peril. Only arrogant authorities want to establish a new clergy-laity chasm. They can avoid this without abdicating primary responsibility for raising up new leadership. I am not referring to the classical concept of suffrage here, but rather the concept of advise and consent. This role recognizes congregational input but eliminates congregational control. No leader should be forced to bless a candidate against his will.

Congregations should be kept informed regarding possible candidates for elder or other ministries. Their input or objections are crucial to the process of ordination. Whether establishing a mentoring council or simply seeking affirmation from the congregation at large, pastors and elders should look to the congregation as part of the discernment and affirmation process.

Many new movements eschew pure democracy when it comes to selecting leaders. The tradition of presbyter approval of candidates has-biblical and historical sanction. Simple election may introduce an element of carnality, which is just as mechanical as the concept of apostolic succession. A genuine agreement (Gr. *sumphoneo)* is the goal of the ordination process. "It seemed good to the Holy Spirit and to us" (Acts 15:28 NIV) – both leaders and led engage in a process to discern the mind of the Lord.

When a congregation has participated in the process and has recognized and experienced the candidate's gifts and calling, then endorses the selection and recognizes and submits to God's will in the choice of their spiritual leaders, tremendous spiritual vitality is released through the process. Universal agreement, to the extent possible, brings health and vitality to the new minister, existing leaders, and congregation. The congregation does not drive the process, but is clearly a witness and participant.

Members should be given the opportunity to express concerns about a given candidate and privately resolve whatever substantial issues there may be, calling on the elders of the church if there is an impasse. If there is a serious interpersonal problem, either it will be resolved or point to issues serious enough to affect the process and selection.

A well-run process will result in the congregation accepting the new pastor's spiritual leadership. By all means the candidate's stature should be enhanced by ordination, not diminished. The health and good order of the church increases. In essence, the relationship has changed – for the better.

Other Issues

Several other issues should be considered. One is: Do we ordain for life? The gifts and calling of God remain regardless of a person's ordained status. It may be useful in moving from place to place to maintain credentials with a synod, council, presbytery, or network. But an actual place of ministry is validated by the community receiving and affected by the ministry. One need not be re-ordained in such cases, but rather installed with the prior ordination recognized, along with an exhortation to stir up the gift of God.

What of order in our churches? Do local churches in emerging movements have two or more primary levels of ministry? That is, are there ruling elders and deacons alongside ministers of Word and sacrament (pastors) who occupy a distinct role? Or does the role of elder carry the same responsibility – the pastoral duties of Word, sacrament, and care or discipline of the flock? The *primus inter pares*, or first among equals model, to me seems more biblical. It places local church elders on level ground with the primary pastor(s) while recognizing the giftedness of the latter.

In new movements, title is giving way to function, and church governments are less hierarchical, more streamlined affairs emphasizing commitment and gifting. This trend may render talk about ordination, office, and order seemingly irrelevant or too traditional. This is good in that it establishes giftedness as the basis of ministry, not title. Nevertheless, it's my belief that when the community recognizes its leader(s) through ordination, the essential elements established in this study lend themselves to stable, healthy congregational life.

Does the church require oversight beyond the local assembly? That is, do we need bishops, presbyteries, or apostolic teams by whatever name (apostle, director, superintendent)? This, of course, depends on the church government embraced by a given body – and a choice about church government must be made. This is true whether that government is a traditional episcopal, presbyterian, or congregational government, or a hybrid, as is often the case in new movements. It seems the question of need (element two) answers this question. Contemporary New Testament churches that may reject the traditional terminology just cited still must wrestle with how the five-fold ministry concept affects their polity in practical ways.

Regardless, it seems the role of oversight is one of function rather than order or title. Claims to lofty authority are often harmful, absent a clear recognition of divine gifting for broad oversight. Numerous successful church plants that relate to one another in a presbytery or network would be an example of such authority. This may be established with a rite of recognition on the part of responsible spiritual leaders. In any event, lofty titles, especially in churches that have abandoned apostolic succession, tend to obscure the humility that should characterize all forms of ministry.

In order to establish community life and to perform functions recognized by the state such as weddings, the believing community must have a method of formally recognizing its spiritual leaders. Ordination in some form is that method.

Nevertheless, there is always the possibility that a God-given calling may not be recognized by existing authorities. And the question may be asked: By what authority do you do these things? The issues raised in considering the six essential elements of ordination in the Bible and history help provide a useful answer.

Chapter Seven
Postscript

The primary methods used to identify biblical and historical patterns of ordination have been examination of biblical texts, historical analysis, and personal interviews with pastors and some regional leaders. Some examination of the practice of ordination in the contemporary church was based on interviews not cited in the body of the work. These are mentioned in the Acknowledgements in the front matter of the book. That process is the "hidden hand" which informs the entire project of this book. They helped create the working hypothesis that every church tradition has an established method of identifying, developing, and setting apart leaders, and that these practices form a pattern across denominational lines.

Attendance at numerous ordination or installation services has informed the project. These events have helped form the working idea of the thesis and to confirm its validity. Of course an isolation of six elements of ordination can be considered artificial. This is especially true since these elements aren't set out in systematic fashion anywhere else. But I believe the concept is upheld in the biblical and historical research contained in this book as well as in contemporary practice.

Issues for Further Consideration

An issue not covered in sufficient detail is candidate qualifications. Further consideration should be given to formal means of spiritual formation and doctrinal instruction. This would include an examination of the role of formal education in the development of leaders with application to how local churches can partner with seminaries or establish in-house training programs.

Evaluation of doctrinal positions is very strong in some communions, including written tests and oral examinations, but weak in others. The contemporary non-denominational movements are quite varied in their effectiveness in this area. Suggestions for definite guidelines would be a helpful addition to this study.

Among the most relevant but potentially contentious issues that this book does not address is the role of gender in candidate selection. I purposely sought to isolate larger patterns of the practice of ordination which apply to all qualified candidates across traditional lines. Ordination of women is addressed by various traditions differently. It was not my intention to visit this issue as it does not directly affect the six-fold pattern itself. Regardless of a movement's stance on women's ordination, the general pattern of essential elements of ordination holds true in each self-contained system. For this reason, the literature review (see appendix) does not explore in any detail material relating to the ordination of women, though a great deal has been written on the subject.

A primary purpose of the book is to provide ordination guidelines for contemporary movements, especially those lacking any traditional practice in this area. A shorter handbook addressing each of these six components for church ordination councils would be a useful tool. Such a publication would include sections on detailed questions concerning the candidate's sense of call and motives, candid recommendations from spiritual leaders familiar with the candidate, guidelines on forming a mentoring team, suggestions for formal studies and doctrinal preparation, suggestions for planning an ordination service, and instruction on including various segments of the leadership and congregation in the entire process.

Additional work on the question of giftedness or supernatural calling as the only or primary criterion for ministry within the church would also be of some use. This affects the concept of the priesthood of all believers and is a source of contention among those who eschew formal tradition or who employ the laying on of hands with little premeditation. This would include traditions which insist the leading of the Spirit alone is sufficient in such matters as choosing pastors. Entire works on, say, Anabaptist, Reformed, Lutheran, or Pentecostal practices from a historical perspective could add substantially to the foundational historical research contained here.

An entire book could be written on the sacramental nature of ordination in Roman Catholicism, and its rejection by Protestants. Grace conferred (or not) by ordination could also be the subject of further study, as well as the practice of prophecy at ordinations and its legitimacy.

Deposition (removal from ministry) of ordained ministers is a field open to exploration as well. Both in historical and contemporary settings, the question of the terms and processes by which deposition is carried out would clarify both historical and contemporary practice. The concept of doctrinal deviation, heresy, or unorthodox practices as a basis for removal, as well as current controversies within church courts of established denominations, is ripe for examination. What doctrinal issues are tolerated or confronted as well as which practices are considered violations of discipline fall under this category.

The relation between ordination and state recognition of clergy/church practices is also an area of practical application. How does ordination affect the authority to perform weddings, and tax exemption for ministers or churches? What about responsibilities for reporting child abuse or the clergy/penitent privilege in counseling relationships? These, of course, vary from state to state and are already the subject of much discussion.

Finally, the role of accountability for ordained pastors or other ministers of the church could be explored. How is oversight provided in the various forms of polity? Suggestions in this area would be especially helpful to new, non-traditional movements. Practical guidelines for such juridical bodies could be fruitful in establishing encouragement, accountability, and discipline.

Conclusion

In examining the process and practice of ordination in the Bible and history, a general pattern across time and traditions has been established. This study offers valuable guidelines for those who want to understand and pursue the practice of ordination in the context of both biblical and traditional principles. Any communion can compare its practices and doctrine of ordination with the principles outlined in this book and benefit from the exercise. New movements will be able to clarify current patterns or establish necessary practices.

Appendix

Literature Review: A discussion of various sources

This study addresses not only the rite of ordination, but the practices surrounding it – that is, the process of identifying, nurturing, and confirming candidates for ministry in the Christian church. A review of current literature shows that the topic of ordination has been explored primarily in journal articles, sections of systematic theologies, and encyclopedia entries. While there are many references to ordination in patristic literature, canon law, confessional statements, and catechisms, there are few monographs dedicated solely to examining the question of ordination.[174] The varied nature of the literature, the sheer number of journal articles, and the breadth of the study require that a review focus on only a sample of the available material.

Journal Articles and Discussions of Rabbinical Practices

Many of the early journal articles on this subject are concerned with the relation of ordination to Old Testament and rabbinical practices. These discussions were launched by the publication of Eduard Lohse's *Die Ordinationen Im Spat-Judentum und im Neuen Testament* (Gottingen, 1951). In it Lohse argued there was a direct relation between Christian ordination and the

---

[174] There are over 2700 entries on ATLA under the heading "Ordination."

rabbinical ordination of Jewish scholars.[175] Later, David Daube's essay in *The New Testament and Rabbinic Judaism* (1956) on the relation between the Hebrew terms *samakh* and *sim* regarding the laying on of hands deepened interest in the connection between Old Testament, rabbinic, and New Testament ordination.

Arnold Eberhardt, in an article entitled "Jewish and Christian Ordination" (1954),[176] forcefully makes the case, contra Lohse, that *semikhah*, the laying on of hands in rabbinic ordination, was not the only ritual form of ordination. He cites a practice of seating rabbinical ordinands known as *hoshebh* (Gr. *kathisai*) as an alternative to the *semikhah* tradition. While Eberhardt acknowledges that the Moses-Joshua event of Numbers 27 is a model (*locus classicus*)[177] for rabbinical ordination, he offers evidence from the New Testament (Moses' chair, Matt. 23:2) and the patristic church (enthronement of bishops) that laying on of hands was *a* ceremonial form of ordination, not *the* ceremonial form. He also argues that Jewish ordination prior to A.D. 70 was as an elder (*zaqen*) in the Sanhedrin. This is opposed to the master-scholar ordination of a disciple that Lohse suggested.[178] Eberhardt sees both the Jewish and Christian rites of ordination as descending separately from the Moses-Joshua paradigm, rather than borrowing from each other.[179]

J. K. Parrat wrote in *The Expository Times* on "The Laying on of Hands in the New Testament. A Re-examination in the Light of Hebrew Terminology" (1969).[180] According to Parrat, the *semikhah* tradition rooted in the Moses-Joshua paradigm is not

---

[175] Arnold Eberhardt, *The Journal of Ecclesiastical History*, October, 1954, Vol. V, No. 2, 125.

[176] Arnold Eberhardt, *The Journal of Ecclesiastical History*, October, 1954, Vol. V, No. 2, 125-138.

[177] Ibid., 130.

[178] Eberhardt also addresses the commissioning of the *shaliah*, or sent one, in relation to New Testament ordination.

[179] Ibid., 138.

[180] J.K. Parratt, "The Laying on of Hands," *The Expository Times,* April 1969, Vol. LXXX, No. 7, 210-214.

the forerunner of New Testament ordination; rather, he argues that *sim*, or blessing, is the basis of New Testament ordination. He does so because, in his view, there is no impartation in New Testament commissioning as in the Numbers 27 account. For Parrat, New Testament ordination is a setting apart by the whole church for a specific task.[181]

Everett Ferguson, in "The Laying on of Hands: Its Significance in Ordination" (1975),[182] recognizes *samakh* as the technical term for ordination in Judaism, but sees *sim* (blessing) as the more likely usage. The basic idea in early Christian ordination was not creating a substitute or transferring authority, but conferring a blessing and petitioning for the divine favor. Blessing, of course, in ancient thought was more than a kindly wish; it was thought of as imparting something very definite (as in the patriarchal blessings of the Old Testament).[183]

For Ferguson, the laying on of hands for blessing was not limited to ordination, but has a multifaceted purpose and meaning, all related to spiritual enrichment of the person receiving prayer. Prayer is as important a component as, if not more important than, the imposition of hands in ordination.[184]

M.C. Sansom, in "Laying on of Hands in the Old Testament" (1983),[185] examines the term *samakh* and argues that the term indicates both transference and acknowledgment or identification. The significance for ordination is that "the laying-on of hands is the official investiture to that task, and we may confidently accept that the hand-laying is connected with the idea of a transference."[186]

Ibid., 218.

[182] Everett Ferguson, "Laying on of Hands: Its Significance in Ordination" *The Journal of Theological Studies,* April, 1975, Vol. XXVI, Part 1, 1-12.

[183] Ibid., 2

[184] Ibid., 10.

[185] M.C. Sansom, "Laying on of Hands in the Old Testament," *The Expository Times,* 1983, Vol. 94, No. 11, 323-326.

[186] Ibid., 325.

Two other articles of note deal with the issue of ordination controversies in Puritan England and the nature of the Free Church doctrine of ministry. Richard L. Greaves, in "The Ordination Controversy and the Spirit of Reform in Puritan England," (1970)[187] examines events in Puritan England from1644 through 1654. During this time leading up to the Cromwellian Protectorate, ordination as a requirement for exercising the right to preach was denounced by many sectarians (Free Church) and defended by more conservative ministers. The rite of ordination was seen as a defense of the status quo and a hindrance to the free moving of the Spirit by one party and a safeguard of order and doctrinal purity by the other.

In relation to ministry and ordination, Edgar Richards in "Is There a Free Church Doctrine of the Ministry?" (1969)[188] argues:

> [I]t has consistently been a Free Church principle concerning the ministry that the inward call of God takes precedence over the official and ceremonial authorization of the Church. Indeed, none of the major Free Churches has regarded the laying on of hands as essential in ordination.[189]

Personal call, parity of all ministries (as opposed to the tiered orders of Episcopal Catholicism), and an acknowledgment of the significance of ordination are part of Richards' argument that "ministry is for service rather than for rule, and that it is subject to the church as a whole, and to be exercised in the service of the Gospel."[190]

---

[187] Richard L. Greaves, "The Ordination Controversy and the Spirit of Reform in Puritan England," *The Journal of Ecclesiastical History,* July, 1970, Vol. XXI, No. 3, 225-240.
[188] Edgar Richards, "Is there a Free Church Doctrine of the Ministry?" *The Expository Times,* May, 1969, Vol. LXXX, No. 8, 242-25.
[189] Ibid., 244.
[190] Ibid., 245.

Patristic Texts

Most of the early patristic texts deal with the results of appointment to church office, rather than the rite of ordination itself. Clement of Rome introduced the concept of succession, which became foundational for the Catholic understanding of ministry.[191] The *Didache* (prior to 120 A.D.)[192] assumes the existence of ordinary (local) ministers (bishops and deacons) as well as traveling apostles, prophets, and teachers, but makes no detailed mention of ordination.[193] Ignatius, Irenaeus, Tertullian, and Cyprian all make reference to the role of the bishop in the life of the church, and the importance of ordained apostolic succession for the sake of unity and sound doctrine.[194] Their teachings contribute to the development of a sacralized ministry. The lack of early texts that explicitly describe the rite of ordination creates some speculation about its development in the early patristic church.[195] This point doesn't eliminate the fact that ministers were in some way recognized and confirmed in their very prominent role in the church.

The first text dealing in detail with the process of ordination is the *Apostolic Tradition (c.* 215) of Hippolytus, presbyter at Rome.[196] Of particular interest is Hippolytus's episcopal ordination

---

[191] This development is addressed in the Introduction.

[192] According to Patrick J. Hamel, *Handbook of Patrology,* (Staten Island, NY: Alba House, 1968), 24. Lightfoot, "(T)he archaic simplicity of its practical suggestions is only consistent with the early infancy of a church. These indications point to the first or the beginning of the second century as the date of the work in its present form." *The Apostolic Fathers,* 122.

[193] "Appoint for yourselves therefore bishops and deacons worthy of the Lord . . . ." in "The Teaching of the Lord to the Gentiles by the Twelve Apostles," in *The Apostolic Fathers,* op. cit., 128.

[194] See Introduction.

[195] So Leon Morris and Alexander Strauch op. cit. footnotes 16 and 17 in Introduction.

[196] "The *Apostolic Tradition* contains the earliest ritual of ordination and it is Roman. There are long liturgical excerpts – it gives a list of ordinations of bishops, priests and deacons . . ." in Hamel, 83.

prayer. The heart of the prayer, which has been revived in Catholic and Episcopal ordination liturgies,[197] is a plea for the outpouring of the Spirit. Mention is made of Jesus' possession of the Spirit and the apostles' reception of the Spirit from Jesus. The clear implication of the prayer is that the bishop's spiritual empowerment is in the same line as that of the apostles – that is, it is in a direct line from Jesus through the apostles. The ordination prayer also petitions for the ability to fulfill pastoral and "high priestly" duties of feeding the flock, propitiating the Lord's countenance, offering holy gifts, remitting sins, giving lots, and "to loose every bond according to the power which thou gavest to the apostles."[198] The episcopal ordination service is thus an empowering with the Spirit to carry out apostolic tasks.

Similar to the *Traditions* are the *Apostolic Constitutions* (a Syrian document *c.*380).[199] This work addresses the ordination of bishops, presbyters, and deacons. "[It] depends on Hippolytus's work and is the most important collection of liturgical laws that has come down from Christian Antiquity." [200] Of note in the *Constitutions* are the character and examination requirements for the offices, especially that of bishop (Book II, secs. i,ii). Character, age, education, and temperament play a role in the selection process, and an examination is required to establish whether the candidate is of blameless character. Sufficient education, meekness, generosity, and an absence of anger are

---

[197] Geoffrey Wainwright, "Some Theological Aspects of Ordination," *Ordination Rites Past and Present*, Wiebe Vos and Geoffrey Wainwright, eds. (Rotterdam: Liturgical Ecumenical Center Trust, 1980), 125. "(H)is prayer for the ordination of a bishop has been taken . . . into the *Pontificale Romanum* of 1968 and the 1977 *Book of Common Prayer* of the Episcopal Church USA."
[198] Quoted in Wainwright, 126. Wainwrigth uses H.B. Porter's translation of Hippolytus's prayer.
[199] Hamel, 83.
[200] Ibid.

necessary qualities.[201] Other character traits are based on I Timothy 3:1ff.[202]

The *Constitutions* restrict "priestly" functions to the presbyters and bishops. "Neither do we permit the laity to perform any of the office belonging to the priesthood; as, for instance, neither the sacrifice, nor baptism, nor the laying on of hands, nor the blessing . . . For such sacred offices are conferred by the laying on of hands of the bishop."[203] In this way the office of bishop and presbyter is further sacralized. Other guidelines and restrictions for the major orders are clarified in the *Constitutions*, including the proper number of bishops for an episcopal ordination (generally three, or at least two).[204]

The decrees of the church councils (early canon law) give some insight into aspects of the process of ordination. Among these are qualifications of ordinands, the position and role of ordaining authorities, the need for examination of candidates, discouragement of neophyte ordination, and how bishops or presbyters may be disciplined or disqualified from office. The Canons of Nicaea (325 A.D.) are representative of the concerns of other councils. "Those who have come from the heathen shall not be immediately advanced to the presbyterate" (Ancient Epitome of Canon II); "A bishop is to be chosen by all the bishops of the province, or at least by three, the rest giving their assent" (Ancient Epitome of Canon IV). "Whoever are ordained without examination, shall be deposed if it be found afterwards that they had been guilty" (Epitome of Canon IX).[205] Other canons deal with the reception of repentant

---

[201] *Constitutions of the Holy Apostles*, eds. Alexander Roberts and James Donaldson, *Ante-Nicene Fathers,* Vol. 7, (Christian Literature Publishing Co., 1886; reprint, Peabody, MA: Hendrickson Publishers, Inc., 1994), 396-399.

[202] Ibid., 397.

[203] Ibid., 429.

[204] Ibid., p. 432. Of particular interest for our purposes are the restrictions on which orders may participate in which ordinations.

[205] "The Canons of the 318 Holy Fathers Assembled in the City of Nice in Bythinia," eds. Philip Schaff and Hebry Wace, *Nicene and Post-Nicene*

schismatic bishops, the geographical locale of the ministries of ordained persons, and similar concerns.[206]

There are four ancient treatises dealing with the call to ministry (the priesthood)[207] and the nature of pastoral ministry in the church. They serve as commentary on the role and expected temperament of priests, as well as instructions to potential candidates for ministry. Three of these treatises spring from a common source; the fourth addresses similar concerns but is an unrelated work. The first three are Gregory Nazianzen's *Second Oration* (362 A.D.), John Chrysostom's *On the Priesthood* (c. 373), and Gregory the Great's *Book of Pastoral Rule* (591). The latter two are both based on the work of Nazianzen. Gregory's *Book of Pastoral Rule* was used as a training manual in pastoral theology in the Middle Ages.[208]

In his *Second Oration*, Gregory Nazianzen explains why he fled from his father's church in Nazianzen to Pontus after being ordained to the priesthood against his will. He uses the opportunity to describe the dignity, obligations, pitfalls, and challenges of the priestly ministry. This serves as the pattern for the works of Chrysostom and Gregory the Great. Chrysostom's work *On the Priesthood,* among other things, discusses the dangers, temptations, dignity, and challenges of the priesthood. He considers

---

Fathers, Vol. 14, Second Series (Charles Scribners Sons, 1900; reprint, Peabody, MA: Hendrickson Publishers, Inc., 1994) 10-11,23.

[206] Ibid., 20,32.

[207] The concept of the ministry as a priesthood (*'ieros)* was introduced early in the patristic era. "In the New Testament itself the concept of 'priest' referred either to the Levites of the Old Testament, now made obsolete, or to Christ, or to the entire church – not to the ordained ministry of the church. But Clement, who was also the first to use the term 'layman {*laikos*},' already spoke of 'priests' and of 'the high priest' and significantly related these terms to the Levitical priesthood; a similar parallel occurred in the *Didache* and in Hippolytus. For Tertullian, the bishop was already 'the high priest,' and for his disciple Cyprian, it was completely natural to speak of a Christian 'priesthood.'" Pelikan, *The Emergence of the Catholic Tradition,* 25.

[208] James Barmby, "The Book of Pastoral Rule, Preface," *Nicene and Post-Nicene Fathers,* vol 12, Second Series, xxxi-xxxii.

in some detail the nature of the preaching ministry as well as the governing tasks of the priesthood.

Of interest for our purposes are Chrysostom's statements concerning those who enter the ministry of the priesthood and those who ordain others. The office should be entered with fear, not by compulsion. Those who ordain the unworthy are as guilty of sin as those who accept the dignity of the office unworthily.

Gregory the Great, Bishop of Rome, in *The Book of Pastoral Rule,* dwells in detail on the motive for accepting ordination to the priesthood, the type of person who ought to come into this position, and who ought not. Gregory then discusses the manner of life of the priest and gives details concerning the care of souls under the minister's charge. In all three works much time is spent on character requirements and possible defects and temptations of those who come into the ministry.

The last work of this genre is *On the Duties of the Clergy* (c. 391) by Ambrose, Bishop of Milan. It is written prior to Gregory's work, and from a different perspective than the others. He had high regard for the ministerial office and wanted his priests to live in a manner worthy of their high calling and to be good examples to the people. "Consequently, he undertook the . . . treatise, setting forth the duties of the clergy, and taking as a model the treatise of Cicero, *De Officiis.* The writer says that his object is to impress upon those whom he has ordained the lessons which he had previously taught them."[209]

Confessions of Faith and Catechisms

Another category of literature dealing with recognition and ordination of candidates for ministry is the confessions of various Christian communions, along with their catechisms for the instruction of the faithful. The confessional statements of major

---

[209] H. De Romestin, "On the Duties of the Clergy, Introduction" *Nicene and Post-Nicene Fathers,* vol. 10, Second Series, xxiii.

Reformation churches are particularly significant. The Lutheran Augsburg Confession (1530) addresses the issue of requirements for ministry on two fronts. One is the restrictions on who may be a minister of word and sacrament. "It is taught among us that no one should teach or preach or administer the sacraments in the church without a regular call" (Article XIV).[210] The second is a relatively long entry under article XXIII that addresses the requirement of celibacy for the priests. "Since God's Word and command cannot be altered by any human vow or laws, our priests and other clergy have taken wives to themselves for these and other reasons."[211]

The Second Helvetic Confession (1566) and the Westminster Confession of Faith (1646) spend little space on the character of the ministry or the nature of ordination. The Westminster Confession does restrict the administration of the sacraments of baptism and the Lord's Supper to a "minister of the Word lawfully ordained" (Article XXVII, iv).[212]

The Anabaptist Dordrecht Confession (1632) is similarly sparing in its discussion of the ministers of the church. Article IX does address the issue, though. "That as the church cannot exist and prosper, nor continue in its structure, without offices and regulations, that therefore the Lord Jesus has Himself. . . appointed and prescribed his offices and ordinances . . . ."[213] This Confession also recognizes the need for ordination of elders with the laying on of hands.[214] The Anglican Thirty-Nine Articles of Religion restrict ministry in the congregation to those lawfully called and sent, and stipulates that one must not take unto himself the ministry of Word or sacrament without such public authority.[215]

---

[210] "The Augsburg Confession" in *Creeds of the Churches,* ed.. John Leith, Third Edition (Atlanta: John Knox Press, 1982), 72.

[211] Ibid., 81.

[212] "The Westminster Confession of Faith," in *Creeds,* 224.

[213] "The Dordrecht Confession," in *Creeds,* 299-300.

[214] Ibid., 301.

[215] "The Thirty-Nine Articles of Religion" in *Creeds,* 274.

A primary source for a medieval Catholic view of the sacerdotal nature of the priesthood is contained in Canon I of the Fourth Lateran Council (1215):

> There is one universal church of believers outside which there is no salvation at all for any. In this church the priest and sacrifice is the same, Jesus Christ Himself, whose body and blood are truly contained in the sacrament of the altar under the figures of bread and wine, the bread having been transubstantiated into His body and the wine into His blood by divine power . . .*and none can effect this sacrament except the priest who has been rightly ordained in accordance with the keys of the Church which Jesus Christ Himself granted to the Apostles and their successors* (emphasis mine).[216]

Some important Catholic publications which address the qualifications of those entering the ministry are *Vatican Council II: The Conciliar and Post Conciliar Documents* (published 1975)[217], and the *Catechism of the Catholic Church* (1995).[218] Sections of these works address all aspects of preparation and recognition for ministry. In the *Documents,* the ancient issue of fitness for the priesthood is discussed in the context of seminary training.

> Notwithstanding the regrettable shortage of priests, due strictness should always be brought to bear on the choice and testing of students. God will not allow his church to lack ministers if the worthy are promoted and those who are not suited to the ministry are guided with fatherly kindness and in due time to adopt another calling[219]

---

[216] Fourth Lateran Council in *Creeds,* 58.

[217] *Vatican II, The Conciliar and Post Conciliar Documents,* Austin Flannery, ed. (Collegeville, MN: Liturgical Press 1975).

[218] *Catechism of the Catholic Church,* (New York: Image Books, 1995).

[219] "Decree on the Training of Priests," *Vatican II,* 712.

The need for spiritual formation as well as doctrinal, intellectual and pastoral formation is also addressed.

> Spiritual formation should be closely associated with doctrinal and pastoral formation, and, with the assistance of the spiritual director in particular, should be conducted in such a way that the students may learn to live in intimate and unceasing union with God the Father, through his Son Jesus Christ, in the Holy Spirit.[220]

Another section of the *Documents,* "Decree on the Ministry and Life of Priests," applies to the life of priests as they carry out their[221] responsibilities after their ordination to the priesthood.

The *Catechism of the Catholic Church* devotes several sections to the nature of the ministry. Most significant for our purpose is the segment on "The Sacrament of Holy Orders." Among the issues addressed are "The Celebration Of The Sacrament," "Who Can Confer This Sacrament?," "Who Can Receive This Sacrament?," and statements on the "Effect Of The Sacrament Of Holy Orders."[222]

A short section of *A Companion to the Greek Orthodox Church,* a series of "essays on essential aspects of Orthodoxy"[223] for an American readership, contains a concise section on the priesthood and ordination.

> The priestly ministry of Christ is perpetuated in the Church by the ministerial priesthood, existing in the three essential ministries of bishop, presbyter and deacon. These are set apart by the grace of ordination to serve the Church; to

---

[220] Ibid., 713.

[221] "Decree on the Life of Priests," *Vatican II*, 863-902.

[222] *Catechism of the Catholic Church,* 438-442. Roman Catholics refer to the rite of ordination as a sacrament.

[223] *A Companion to the Greek Orthodox Church,* ed. Fotios K Listas (New York: Department of Communication Greek Orthodox Archdiocese of North and South America, 1984), ix.

preach, teach and shepherd the people of God; to celebrate the sacred mysteries; to preserve correct doctrine; and to keep the body united in the love of Christ. The ministerial priesthood belongs to the very essence and structure of the Church, having been established by the Lord himself. The gifts and functions once given to the Apostles are transmitted to the ordained ministers through the mystery of the priesthood in the rites of ordination.

The Bishops are the successors to the Apostles, the Chief shepherds and administrators of the Church and the guardians and teachers of the true faith. They are also the celebrants and ministers of the mystery of the priesthood. While the right to choose the ministers of the Church belongs to all the clergy and the people, the bishop alone has the right to ordain and to appoint ministers and to consecrate churches. As a sign of the collegiality of the episcopacy, three bishops (or at least two with the consent of a third) ordain a bishop. In all other ordinations, one bishop suffices.[224]

Again, we see the perceived ancient origin of the practice of ordination and the belief that unity and sound doctrine are preserved by a properly executed ordination in apostolic succession.

Statements of the Major Reformers

Each of the major reformers had great interest in addressing the nature of the ministry, and how one is qualified, appointed, or recognized. Their statements, of course, included comments on the practice of ordination. Luther (cited in Chapter One) was most vehement in his criticism of the rite of ordination as inherited from Catholicism. Calvin had a very developed view of qualifications for pastoral ministry, also quoted in the introductory chapter.

---

[224] Alciviadis C. Calivas, "The Sacramental Life of the Orthodox Church," in *A Companion to the Greek Orthodox Church,* 48.

His views are expounded in great detail in the first nine chapters of Book IV of the *Institutes*. Later in Book IV, he expresses his objections to the Catholic sacrament of ordination:

> In regard to the true office of presbyter, which was recommended to us by the lips of Christ, I willingly give it [ordination] that place [a sacrament]. For in it there is a ceremony which, first, is taken from the Scriptures; and, secondly, is declared by Paul to be not empty or superfluous, but to be a faithful symbol of spiritual grace (I Tim. 4:14). My reason for not giving a place to [it] is because it is not ordinary or common to all believers, but is a special rite for a certain function. But while this honor is attributed to the Christian ministry, Popish priests may not plume themselves upon it. Christ ordered dispensers of his gospel and his sacred mysteries to be ordained, not sacrificers to be inaugurated, and his command was to preach the gospel and feed the flock, not to immolate victims.[225]

English Puritan Presbyterian views are expressed in *The Book of Discipline 1587*, which was first openly published in the English language in 1644[226] at the Westminster Assembly. This work established some guidelines for a Presbyterian understanding of ordination:

> The ministers of public charges in every particular church ought to be called and appointed to their charges by a lawful ecclesiastical calling, such as hereafter is set down....No man can be lawfully called to public charge in the church, but he that is fit to discharge the same. And none is to be accounted fit, but he that is endued with the common gifts of all the

---

[225] *Institutes, IV, xix, 28.*

[226] It was composed in Latin as *Ecclesiasticae Disciplnae Explicatio. The Reformation of the Church,* ed. Iain Murray (London: Banner of Truth trust, 1965), 177.

godly; that is, with faith and a blameless life: and further also, with those that are proper to that ministry wherein he is to be used, and necessary for the executing of the same; whereupon for trial of those gifts some convenient way and examination is to be used.

The party to be called must first be elected, then he is to be ordained to that charge whereunto he is chosen, by the prayers of that church whereunto he is to be admitted; the mutual duties of him and of the church, being before laid open.... In their examination it is specially to be taken heed unto, that they are apt to teach, and tried men, not utterly unlearned, nor newly planted and converted to the faith.[227]

The Book of Discipline here emphasizes that ministers are 1) to fulfill their ministry in a specific setting;[228] 2) that they are to be tested, examined and adjudged as fit and gifted for the calling; 3) to be appointed by the election of the church body which they are to serve; 4) not novices; 5) duly charged and ordained.[229]

A work which explores the thought of reformer Martin Bucer (b. 1491) is *The Ecclesiastical Offices in the Thought of Martin Bucer* (1996), by Willem van't Spijker.[230] This work goes into great detail concerning Catholic, pre-Reformation and Reformation thought concerning ecclesiastical office. Of particular interest for our purposes are the sections on appointment, supervision, and training for ministry, including the manner in which candidates are chosen for their offices.

---

[227] "The Book of Discipline," Iain Murray, ed. *The Reformation of the Church,* 178.

[228] This is probably an indictment of the benefice system where ordinands often did not take the charge committed to them, but received financial benefit from the appointment.

[229] This list emerges as part of the essential characteristics of the ordination process.

[230] Wilem van't Spijker, *Ecclesiastical Offices in the Thought of Martin Bucer,* John Vriend, and Lyle D. Bierma, trans. (Leiden: E.J. Brill, 1996).

Systematic and Pastoral Theologies

Many systematic and pastoral theologies devote some space to the doctrine and practice of ordination. One of the most helpful is *The Study of Liturgy* (1978). Though not a systematic theology *per se,* it is a study on the historical development of liturgical practices, including ordination. The section entitled "Ordination" covers a spectrum of issues from New Testament and early ordination rites through medieval, Reformation, and contemporary practices. This section focuses primarily on the rite and practice of ordination rather than questions of recognition, nurture, and confirmation of candidates for ministerial office. As a discussion of the development of the doctrine, it is invaluable.[231]

Thomas Oden's *Pastoral Theology: Essentials of Ministry* (1983) contains two chapters on the issue of calling and ordination, which are outstanding for succinctness and grasp of the issues involved with identification, nurture, and confirmation. Separate headings address the concept of inward call[232] and outward call.

> The call to ministry requires not only a private, inward, intuitive feeling that one is called by God to ministry; if we had only that, we would invite the abuses of self-assertive, subjective, individualistic self-righteousness. To avoid these abuses, it also requires the affirmation of the visible, believing community.[233]

In fact, Oden's *Pastoral Theology* addresses the concerns of this work so pointedly that several additional quotes are in order. On the role of the community, he speaks of the work of the ordination committee.

---

[231] Jones, Cheslyn, Waiwright, Geoffrey, and Yarnold, Edward, eds. *The Study of Liturgy.* New York: Oxford University Press, 1978, pp. 289-349.

[232] The concept of inward call surfaces in the literature of every age.

[233] Thomas Oden, *Pastoral Theology: Essentials of Ministry,* (San Francisco: Harper Collins Publishers, 1983) 20-21.

The agent by which the external call is made is the visible church – that means fallible, ordinary people in the living body of Christ – through a duly authorized pre-ordination processes....These fallible people are specifically asked not to 'ordain suddenly' (I Tim. 5:22). Hasty, reckless ordinations are prohibited both by specific biblical injunction and tradition (cf. First Council of Nicaea, 325, NPNF 2nd, vol. 14, p. 10).[234]

Oden asks about the necessity and meaning of ordination. Concerning the latter he states, "The effective inner meaning of ordination is the earnest intercession of the church, invoking the Spirit to empower and bless this ministry. This internal side is manifested externally by a visible event: the imposition of hands. The intercession asks God for a continuing endowment of these gifts and for the abiding presence of the Holy Spirit" (Cyprian, ANF, vol. 5, pp. 483 ff., 491 ff.).[235]

Millard Erickson's *Readings in Christian Theology* (1979) contains several entries which examine the concerns of ordination under the heading "The Nature of the Church."[236] Though these entries mostly address church polity, ordination is broached of necessity. Leon Morris, in "Nature and Government of the Church (Episcopalian View)," examines the traditional view of succession and ordination.[237] Louis Berkhof, in an excerpt "The Government of the Church" (taken from his *Systematic Theology*, in Erickson), discusses internal and external call and ordination under the heading "The Calling of the Officers and Their Induction into Office."[238]

---

[234] Ibid., 20.

[235] Ibid., 30.

[236] *Readings in Christian Theology,* Volume 3, ed. Millard J.Erickson, (Grand Rapids: Baker Book House, 1979), 311-354.

[237] Morris puts forward the surprising view, for an Anglican, that ordination may not have been the vehicle of preserving succession until the time of Augustine, p. 314.

[238] Louis Berkhof, "The Government of the Church," in *Readings in Christian Theology,* 326.

Both the officers and the ordinary members of the church have a part in it. That the officers have a guiding hand in it, but not to the exclusion of the people….Says Dr. Hodge, 'Ordination is the solemn expression of the judgment of the Church, by those appointed to deliver such judgment, that the candidate is truly called of God to take part in the ministry, thereby authenticating to the people the divine call'…It may briefly be called a public acknowledgement and confirmation of the candidate's calling to this office.[239]

And while Protestants regard ordination "as a Scriptural rite and one that is entirely appropriate, they do not regard it as absolutely essential."[240]

Compendiums and Anthologies

Some of the most helpful works include compendiums of journal articles or essays, some compiled from papers written for conferences. On the process of ordination itself, *Ordination Rites Past and Present*, edited by Wiebe Vos and Geoffrey Wainwright, is the most informative about the ordination ceremony. The essays, presented at the 1979 Congress of *Societas Liturgica*, cover a gamut from how ordination is viewed today, to Jewish, New Testament, and ancient rites of ordination, as well as the practices of the Reformers through to contemporary changes.

Two similar collections address the role of the bishop in today's episcopal communions. They are *Bishops but What Kind?* (1982), edited by Peter Moore[241], and *The Unifying Role of the Bishop* (1972), edited by Edward Schillebeeckx.[242] Articles in both

---

[239] Ibid., 326.

[240] Ibid., 327.

[241] *Bishops But What Kind: Reflections on Episcopacy*, ed. Peter Moore (London: SPCK, 1982).

[242] *The Unifying Role of the Bishop*, ed. Edward Schillebeeckx, (New York: Heder and Herder, 1972).

collections address the role of the bishop in ordination or the role of ordination in making a bishop. Another similar work, written from a generically episcopal perspective, is *To Be A Priest* (1975), edited by Robert Terwilliger and Urban T. Holmes III.[243]

Finally, collections from a symposium on *The Experience of Ordination* (1979), edited by Kenneth Wilson,[244] records the subjective reflections of various ordinands on the process and effect of ordination in their lives and ministry.

Monographs

Among monographs on the subject, the most comprehensive is Marjorie Warkentin's *Ordination: A Bibical-Historical View* (1982). The focus of this book is the rite of ordination as expressed through the laying on of hands in the Bible and history. The book begins with the actual practice of the laying on of hands in the Bible and history. Warkentin traces its use from Old Testament roots through the New Testament and church history, focusing primarily on the development of the doctrine and practice of ordination. She comes to the conclusion that the practice of ordination as we know it has dubious validity. Warkentin's survey is well-researched and helpful on the development of the rite and practice of ordination. I find her conclusions somewhat strained in places.[245]

---

[243] *To Be A Priest: Perspectives on Vocation and Ordination*, eds. Robert E. Terwiliger and Urban T. Holmes, III (Seabury Press: New York, 1975).

[244] *The Experience of Ordination*, ed. Kenneth Wilson (London: Epworth Press, 1979).

[245] For instance, in her discussion of possible ordination passages in I and II Timothy, she sees a conscious Pauline repetition of the Moses-Joshua relationship with Timothy. Thus, the references are non-repeatable and do not serve as a pattern for the Christian Church. The reference in I Tim. 5:22 "Do not be hasty in the laying on of hands, and do not share in the sins of others. Keep yourself pure," widely viewed as a reference to the danger of improper or premature ordination is seen as a warning against failure to fully observe Jewish sacrificial rituals such as the fulfillment of a Nazirite vow.

Another monograph devoted entirely to the practice of ordination is Alton H. McEachern's *Set Apart for Service: Baptist Ordination Practices* (1980). This book is a very practical survey of the meaning and methods of ordination, including an historical and trans-denominational analysis from a Southern Baptist perspective. As to be expected, written from a Free Church viewpoint, it is anti-clerical.

In his view, the New Testament practice of ordination, if it is to be called that, was highly practical. It was not for the elevation of the ordinand, but for the edification of the church and evangelistic outreach . . . There is little reason to believe that the New Testament Church viewed its officers as a superior class of believers (clergy vs. laity). This was a distortion which came later in church history. [246]

McEachern emphasizes several other areas often repeated in other literature, especially of a Free Church nature. "The New Testament pattern of ordination appears to be more functional than professional . . . Ordination is official recognition by a local congregation and its sister churches that the Holy Spirit has called out certain persons to function in specialized ministry within the church and churches . . . Ordination was an outward confirmation of the inward call and obvious gifts of ministry already possessed . . . . ."[247]

Another monograph dealing exclusively with the issue of ordination is Mark Chaves' *Ordaining Women: Culture and Conflict in Organizations* (1997). This work, of course, deals almost exclusively with the issue of the ordination of women. The bibliography provides many sources on the question of ordination as well as the issue of women's ordination.

Other books devote portions of their studies to the practice of ordination. A contemporary work written from a Free Church perspective is Alexander Strauch's *Biblical Eldership: An Urgent*

---

[246] Alton H. McEachern, *Set Apart for Service: Baptist Ordination Practices,* (Nashville: Broadman Press, 1980), 18.
[247] Ibid., 21.

Call to Restore Biblical Church Leadership (Revised and Expanded 1995, 2016). This is actually a comprehensive discussion of the concept of church office and the manner in which one is fitted for it. It includes a discussion of setting church leadership into place.

In Chapter 14, "Appointment of Elders," Strauch offers his view of ordination (a term he eschews for the preferred "appointment"). He cites six elements of the appointment process. They are desire, qualification, selection, examination, installation, and prayer.[248] Strauch's thesis is that all elders should have a pastoral role and qualifications. "All pastor elders are to be fully qualified, formally examined, and publicly installed into office."[249]

Several points of importance for our purposes include Strauch's recommendation that the existing elders normally take the lead in the appointment process, that the potential elder have a definite desire to shepherd the flock, and the necessity that the individual be the choice of God.[250] *Biblical Eldership* rejects the Reformation view that the ministry of Word and sacrament is reserved to the ordained ministry. "No one needs to be ordained to preach Christ or administer the ordinances. All such concepts are foreign to New Testament apostolic churches."[251] Strauch, in agreement with many others but contrary to Warkentin, sees the references in I and II Timothy as pertaining to the practice of appointment (ordination) of church officers.[252] Strauch concludes, "So formal installation is an official starting point. Furthermore, the formal installation of an elder by the laying on of hands would communicate to the new elder the approval, blessing, prayers, recognition, and fellowship of the church."[253]

A similar, but less known, contemporary Free Church (the

---

[248] Strauch, *op. cit.,* 277.

[249] Ibid., 277.

[250] Ibid., 278, 280.

[251] Ibid., 287.

[252] Ibid., 287.

[253] Ibid., 288.

term New Testament Church is probably preferable) treatment is James Garrett's *New Testament Church Leadership* (1996). Chapter 10 is entitled "Ordination in the New Testament Church." This chapter concludes with a segment on practical application.

> No leader in the New Testament Church, whether of the special class or other leaders, came into ministry at his own suggestion. All were *recruited* or called to ministry by ecclesiastical authorities or by a sovereign act of God. There is no example of someone's coming to leadership with the statement, "I feel called to become a pastor, missionary, etc." With the exception of the elders chosen in Acts 14:23, those installed in ministry roles were experienced, usually mentored, and proven. Thus, we conclude that God may stir someone's heart toward a particular ministry, but a 'call' is not consummated until it is recognized and verified by those in authority (local elders or one in an apostolic church planting ministry).[254]

Miroslav Volf in his study of ecclesiology, *After Our Likeness* (1998), devotes a subsection to a discussion of the recognition of church office through ordination. In a section addressing our concerns, he states:

> [O]rdination is to be understood *as a public reception of a charisma given by God and focused on the local church as a whole* . . . It would, of course, be inadequate to view this reception as something simply external to the charisma of office, a mere acknowledgment of an already existing situation. As already explained, ecclesial reception is an important dimension of the *bestowal* of the charismata; this applies to the charismata of office as well. Ordination is a public and solemn conclusion to a much longer ecclesial

---

[254] James W. Garrett, *New Testament Church Leadership,* (Tulsa: Doulos Publishing, 1996), 199-200.

process of reception, one that as a whole is part of the constitution of the charisma of office itself. It follows that ordination is essentially a divine-human act.

Because the ministry of officeholders involves the entire local church, the charismata of office require reception by the entire congregation. Thus, in the second place, *ordination is an act of the entire local church led by the Spirit of God,* and not simply of one stratum within the church perpetuating itself through the very institution of ordination.[255]

Volf goes on to recognize that ordination is not always to a lifelong task, and that ordination, in his understanding of it, is always bound to a certain local church, though wider recognition of one's ordination may exist in a given community of local churches.[256] Volf sees in the election of candidates for ordination[257] a matter of tremendous significance for congregations.

With regard to the electoral process, understanding election as reception means abandoning the schema according to which people choose between various candidates by means of simple acts of the will . . .Election is the beginning of the formal and explicit ecclesial reception of a charisma of office, but it is also the end of the informal and implicit reception . . . Understanding election as reception means starting theologically with the priority of divine action . . .Through this interactional electoral process, the members of a church single out those whom *God* has already called (see Acts 13:2). Nor can this be otherwise if ordination is not to be reduced to the delegation of power by the congregation. If God does not stand at the beginning of

---

[255] Volf, 249.

[256] Ibid., 250-251.

[257] The right of congregations to choose their own ministers was of highest importance to the Reformers.

the explicit process of reception, neither can God be found at its end .[258]

One of the most comprehensive discussions of the recognition, nurture, and confirmation of church leadership from a New Testament perspective is by Kevin Giles, *Patterns of Ministry Among the First Christians* (1989). Speaking of the tension between charisma and office, Giles states:

> [Paul] understands that the church will recognize as leaders those whom God is regularly using to build up the community. When a significant ministry was exercised over a period of time by one person, and the community had come to recognize him/her as a leader, important elements in the concept of office were present. In other words the natural outcome of regularly exercised Spirit-initiated ministries was the emergence of office-bearers in the church."[259]

Giles introduces a seven-fold pattern of the development of office in the early church beyond the era of the NT church:

1. An element of permanency.
2. Some degree of recognition by the church. (These two things are present when certain people can be designated by a title that describes the work they do.)
3. A position somewhat apart from other members of the church. (This would involve respect and authority).
4. Payment for service.
5. Authorization. (Letters of commendation or specific commissioning, e.g. the laying on of hands.)
6. Establishment by law. (The securing of position by ecclesiastical statute.)

---

[258] Ibid., 256.
[259] Kevin Giles, (Melbourne, Australia: Collins Dove, 1989), 18-19.

7. The sacralization of the position. (Priestly status is given to the office bearer.)[260]

Giles's eighth chapter is entitled "From Commissioning for Ministry to Ordaining for Life." Here he lays out his theology of ordination most explicitly. He contrasts the study of ministries in the early church with the study of the doctrine of ordination. When speaking of ministries, "[t]here is debate on some issues and uncertainty on others, but no confusion about what is being discussed. The case is different with ordination: here the fog is almost impenetrable. There is no agreement on what the concept involves."[261]

Giles sees ordination as a question of leadership and legitimation and uses Max Weber's categories of leadership to discuss the legitimation of Christian ministry. He adjusts these categories somewhat into charismatic, traditional, and sacral/rational. Giles sees the primary New Testament validation of ministry to be recognition of charismatic gifts.

> Whether or not the laying on of hands was involved [in Acts 14:23], these men were appointed to office in a solemn religious setting. Whatever authority they possessed already, through age or charisma or both, was supplemented when the great missionary apostles set them apart for their special work. By this action, the elders' authority was sacrally legitimated in the eyes of the whole community.

> These texts [1 Tim. 4:14; 2 Tim. 1:6] are commonly read as evidence that the Pastorals bear witness to a church order in which, through the laying on of hands, the *charisma* of office is conveyed. If this is the case, the laying on of hands no longer supplements charismatic legitimation but in its own right legitimates.[262]

---

[260] Ibid., 17.
[261] Ibid., 173.
[262] Ibid., 189.

For Giles, the concept of laying on of hands (ordination) becomes the primary means of legitimation of ministry. In this way the primacy of charismatic endowment became virtually forgotten, at least in the post- apostolic church.[263] The increase in significance of the rite of ordination contributed to a sacralization of the episcopal and presbyter's office, thus giving them official functions denied to other Christians.[264] This ultimately led to the result in the Middle Ages that "[i]t came to be believed that in the sacrament of ordination an *ontological* change was effected through the laying on of hands by a bishop. This meant the clergy were not simply functioning as priests in the exercise of their ministry, but were in effect a completely separate and holy class of men. By ordination an indelible character was imprinted on their souls"[265] (emphasis mine).

According to Giles, the Reformers struck a blow against this sacralization but did not remove it completely. "They thus maintained a clear distinction between ordained and unordained: clergy and laity . . .at least as far as Calvin was concerned, it depended on a specific and personal divine call and enabling – which in ordination, the church simply recognized."[266]

Giles concludes his segment on ordination with the following observations for the emerging Free Churches:

> Some public form of sacral/rational legitimation of those already legitimated charismatically is essential once a church settles down and the inevitable process of institutionalization is underway. It is our argument, however, that the church was gravely mistaken in coming to think that ordination itself bestowed the gifts of ministry; or that it conveyed exclusive powers and created a uniquely holy and separate class of persons . . . What is needed is a theology that encourages

---

[263] Ibid., 194.
[264] Ibid., 194-5
[265] Ibid., 195.
[266] Ibid., 195.

all Christians to be active in ministry, yet recognizes and endorses the distinctive contribution of those called to ongoing communal leadership.[267]

Denominational Booklets, Pamphlets, Church Orders

Many churches have published handbooks, pamphlets, or church orders that address the concept of recognition, nurture, and confirmation of one's call to ministry. Normally this process culminates in ordination. A select survey of some of these materials clarifies the nature of these publications.

The Evangelical Lutheran Church in America publishes *What Shall I Say? Discerning God's Call to Ministry* (1995).[268] This publication, designed to help individuals discern a personal call to the ministry, explores the issues of giftedness, officially recognized ministries of the Lutheran Church, and the nature of pastoral ministry. Other forms of ministry are explored, such as rostered lay ministry and diaconal ministry. A detailed process of examining oneself for a call to ordained ministry is described, which includes worship, study, and prayer with the church; talking with people the candidate knows; exploring work possibilities in and out of the church; discerning gifts for ministry; and responding to God's call in obedience. The candidacy process is then explained.

Another Lutheran publication, *Called by God, Responding with a Life of Service* (no date) is actually in the form of a pamphlet. It succinctly covers the call to ministry, gifting for ministry, varieties of ministry (order), preparation, candidacy, and placement. The pamphlet concludes with a challenge to consider whether one is actually being called into ministry in the Lutheran Church.

---

[267] Ibid., 197.

[268] Madelyn H. Busse and A. Craig Settlage, eds. *What Shall I Say? Discerning God's Call to Ministry.* (Evangelical Lutheran Church in America, 1995).

The Book of Discipline of the Mennonite Church (1996)[269] provides a detailed description of requirements for ordained ministry. These include ethics and accountability requirements and detailed instructions regarding matters such as accountability, impartiality, sexual ethics, confidentiality, conflict resolution, and ethical behavior after leaving a pastoral assignment. There is also a section on polity, which describes order, forms of recognition, and ordination policies. These include defining the ordaining authority and how candidates are appointed to specific ministries.

Another Mennonite publication is *Confession of Faith in a Mennonite Perspective* (1995).[270] Articles 15 and 16 deal with "Church Ministry and Leadership" and "Church Order and Unity." These include declarations on the role of the church in the calling, equipping, and placing of church leadership. "Church Order" includes a description of the decision-making process, which includes recognizing and nurturing new leadership.

A third Mennonite publication, *The Ministers' Manual*, includes a segment on "Calling and Setting Apart of Leaders." The ordination process includes confirmation of call, affirming of gifts, identifying the one set apart for a "priestly" role within the congregation, and entrusting the office of ministry to the one being ordained.

The Red Book: *Guidelines for the Ordination Process (The Commission on Ministry, the Episcopal Diocese of Southwest Virginia)* prepared specifically for the Diocese of Southwest Virginia, is a practical, hands-on guide to the ordination process in the Episcopal Church. It gives in detail all the steps both initiating and leading to the process of ordination. In addition to outlining the steps to ordination, specific forms or reports to be filed with the bishop's office are included in the appendices. These include reports of the discernment group and the rector,

---

[269] Everett J. Thomas, ed. *The Book of Discipline of the Mennonite Church*. (Newton, KA: Faith and Life Press, 1996).

[270] *Confession of Faith in a Mennonite Perspective* (Scottdale, PA: Herald Press, 1995).

the recommendation of the vestry, biographical data, a financial statement, and a certificate of recommendation.

The Assemblies of God published a position paper on Ordination in 1977[271] in conjunction with a booklet entitled "Theological and Functional Dimensions of Ordination." This is a thorough exploration of the types of ministry practiced in this movement, qualifications for ministry, the purpose and benefits of ordination, and numerous practical considerations concerning the issue.

Conclusion

Several issues of importance emerge in the literature review. Among them are the issue of God's sovereignty in the process of identifying and confirming potential ministers and the role of the congregation in recognizing and receiving a spiritually gifted candidate. Related to these are the importance of the individual sense of personal calling and the role of the community in confirming that subjective experience. Added to these is the place of existing spiritual leadership in identifying and confirming emerging ministries, along with their role in the actual rite of ordination. The recognition of local ordination in the wider church, along with the question of ritual impartation of spiritual gifts, is a recurring theme in the literature. It is often discussed in contrast to simple recognition of the existing gifts of the candidate.

The actual purpose of ordination has also emerged as a question for discussion. What ministries are legitimated or enhanced by ordination? Is there an ordination to an "at-large" ministry and, if so, under what circumstances? What about training, whether formal education or a mentoring process? The character of the ordinand emerges as a significant issue in some of the literature, especially the recent New Testament Church (Free

---

[271] "Theological and Functional Dimensions of Ordination," (Springfield, MO: Gospel Publishing House, 1977).

Church) discussions of church government.[272] Further, does the relationship between the ordinand and congregation change? Are there official functions, prerogatives, or responsibilities assigned to the minister that he did not possess before? Is there a respect or obedience due?

Finally, and importantly, does emphasis on the rite of ordination contribute to the sacralization of the pastoral/episcopal office and thus contribute to the clergy/laity distinction to the detriment of the priesthood of all believers? These are just some of the issues raised and discussed in the literature. It has been my intention to address many of these questions in distilling these thoughts to identify *essential* elements of ordination in the Bible and history.

---

[272] The NT church movement discussions are based primarily, if not solely, on NT texts regarding fitness for ministry. Other publications include these elements, but include references to historical practice.

Bibliography

Balmforth, Henry. *The Christian Priesthood*, London, SPCK, 1963

Baldwin, Joyce G. *1 and 2 Samuel An Introduction and Commentary*. Tyndale Old Testament Commentaries, D.J. Wiseman, ed. Downers Grove, Inter-Varsity Press, 1988

Barrett, C.K. *Acts, Vol I*, The Internatoinal Critical Commentary, J.A. Emerton, C.E.B. Cranfield, G.N. Stanton, eds. (Edinburgh, Tand T clark, 1994.

Henry Bettenson, ed. *Documents of the Christian Church,* Second Edition. London: Oxford University Press, 1963.

The Book of Discipline of the United Methodist Church, 2000. Nashville, TN: The United Methodist Publishing House, 2000.

Brown, Raymond. *Priest and Bishop Biblical Reflections.* New York: Paulist Press, 1970

Brueggemann, Walter. *1 Kings*, Knox Preaching Guides, John H. Hayes, ed. Atlanta: John Knox Press, 1982

John Calvin, *Institutes of the Christian Religion,* IV, ii, 2.

Campbell, R. Alastair. *The Elders: Seniority within Earliest Christianity.* Edinburg: T and T Clark, 1994.

Daube, David. *The New Testament and Rabbinic Judaism.* New York: Arno Press, 1956, rpt. 1973.

John Dillenberger, ed. *Martin Luther, Selections from His Writings.* Garden City, NY: Anchor Books, 1961.

Dix, Gregory and Henry Chadwick, eds. *The Treatise on the Apostolic Tradition of St. Hippolytus of Rome.* London: Alban Press, 1938, rev. 1992.9

Elwell, Walter. *Evangelical Dictionary of Theology.* Grand Rapids: Baker Book House, 1984.

Millard Erickson, ed. *Readings in Christian Theology.* Grand Rapids: Baker Book House, 1979.

Fee, Gordon, 1 and 2 Timothy, New international Biblical Commentary, Peabody, MA Hendrikson, 1984

Garrett, James. *New Testament Church Leadership.* Tulsa, OK: Doulos Publishing, 1996.

Gavin, F. *The Jewish Antecedents of the Christian Sacraments.* New York: Ktav Publishing House, Inc. 1969.

Giles, Kevin. *Patterns of Ministry Among the First Christians Second Edition, Revised.,* Eugene, OR: Cascade Publishers, 2017.

Gordon, Robert P. *I and II Samuel A Commentary.* Grand Rapids: Zondervan Publishing House, 1986.

Harris, R. Laird, Gleason L. Archer, and Bruce K. Waltke, eds. *Theological Wordbook of the Old Testament, Vol. II.* Chicago: Moody Bible Institute, 1980.

Johnson, Luke Timothy. *The First and Second Letters to Timothy*, The Anchor Bible. New York, Doubleday, 2001.

Jones, Cheslyn, Geoffrey Wainwright, and Edward Yarnold, eds. *The Study of Liturgy*. New York: Oxford University Press, 1978.

Jones, G.H. 1 and 2 Kings, Vol. I. The New Century Bible Commentary, Ronald E. Clements, Matthew Black, eds. Grand Rapids: William B. Eerdmans Publishing Co., 1984.

Kittel, Gerhard, ed., Geoffrey Bromiley, trans., *Theological Dictionary of the New Testament*. Grand Rapids: Eerdmans Publishing Co., 1965.

Knight, George W. *Commentary on the Pastoral Epistles*, New International Greek Testament Commentary, Grand Rapids: Wiliam B. Eerdmans, 1992

Leith, John H., ed. *Creeds of the Churches, A Reader in Christian Doctrine from the Bible to the Present*. Third Edition, Atlanta: John Knox Press, 1982.

Levine, Baruch. *Numbers 21-36*, The Anchor Bible. New York, Doubleday, 2000.

Lightfoot,J.B., and J.R. Harmer, eds *The Apostolic Fathers*. London: Macmillan and Co., 1891; reprint, Grand Rapids: Baker Book House, 1956.

Milgrom, Jacob. *Numbers*. The JPS Torah Commentary. Philadelphia: The Jewish Publication Society, 1990

Pelikan, Jaroslav. *The Emergence of the Catholic Tradition (100-600)*, Vol. 1, *The Christian Tradition: A History of the*

Development of Doctrine. Chicago: University of Chicago Press, 1971.

Reid, John K.S. "The Biblical Doctrine of the Ministry," Scottish Journal of Theology Occasional Papers, No. 4. Edinburgh, Scotland: Oliver and Boyd Ltd., 1955.

Seabury, William Jones. *An Introduction to the Study of Ecclesiastical Polity,* Second Edition. New York: R.W. Crothers, 1900.

Spijker, Wlliam van't. *The Ecclesiastical Offices in the Thought of Martin Bucer,* trans. John Vriend, Lyle D. Bierma. New York: E.J. Broll, 1996

Strauch, Alexander. *Biblical Eldership An Urgent Call to Restore Biblical Church Leadership,* Revised. Littleton, CO: Lewis and Roth, 1995.

Terwilliger, Robert E. and Urban T. Holmes, eds. *To Be a Priest: Perspectives on Vocation and Ordination.* New York: The Seabury Press, 1985.

Volf, Miroslav. *After Our Likeness: The Church as the Image of the Trinity.* Grand Rapids: Wm. B. Eerdmans, 1998

Vos, Wiebe and Geoffrey Wainwright, eds. *Ordination Rites: Papers Read at the 1979 Congress of Societas Liturgica.* Rotterdam: Liturgical Ecumenical Center, 1980.

Warkentin, Marjorie. *Ordination: A Biblical-Historical View.* Grand Rapids: William B. Eerdmans Publishing Co., 1982.

Wilson, Kenneth. *The Experience of Ordination.* London: Epworth Press, 1979.

Zaragoza, Edward C. *No Longer Servants, but Friends: A Theology of Ordained Ministry.* Nashville: Abingdon Press, 1999.

Printed in the United States
By Bookmasters